With Only Five Plums: The Time Before

Story by Terry Eisele
Art by Jonathon Riddle
Cover by John Novak

This 2013 edition is published by CreateSpace.

www.terryeisele.com

Cover design and art by John Novak.

www.novakarts.com

ISBN-13: 978-1483991146

ISBN-10: 1483991148

Dedication

This book is for A_____way in 2006,
and her family, as v_____uffered at the
hands those who ha_____nd steal their
homeland for centur_____

Introduction

The story you are about to read is based on actual events. The narrator, Anna Nesporova, lived through many of the things described here. Did she personally experience everything presented within these pages? No. Did the people living in this part of the world at this time suffer through these horrors and others? Most certainly. Knowing which events from this story actually occurred in her life and which were created in the service of this narrative is less important than understanding that all of these events happened to large swaths of the European population. For readers who desire to know the "real story" of Anna and the village of Lidice, a wealth of traditional historical material exists. But for readers who want to experience a more human narrative, there is With Only Five Plums: The Time Before.

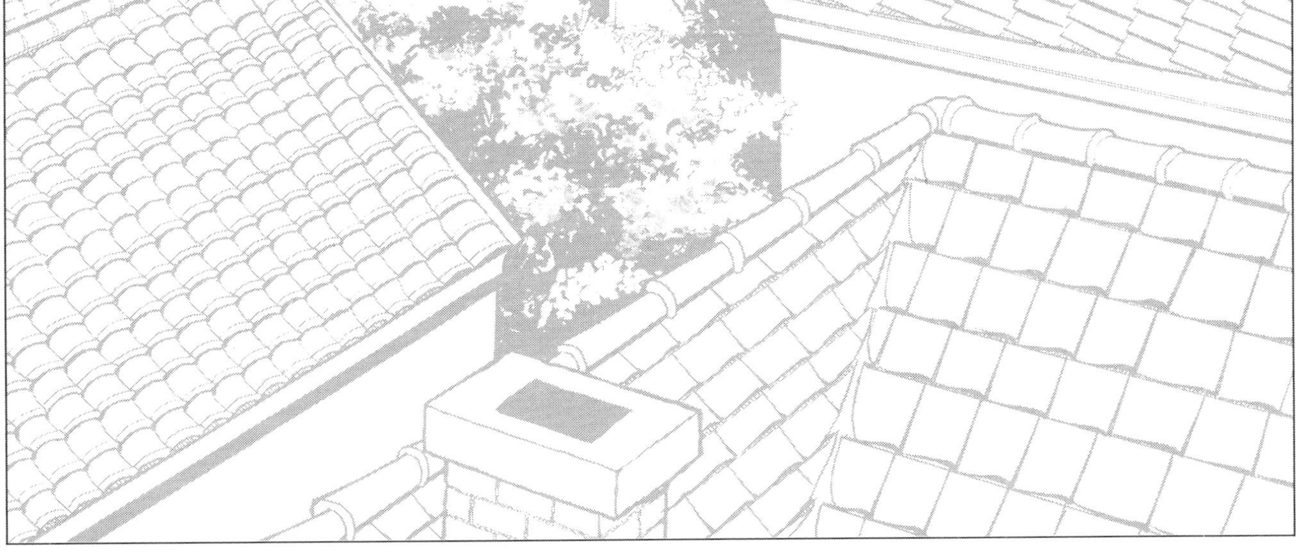

The Far-off Village

We had not heard your name, Lidice;
Till your heart's blood was shed,
You had no fame to reach us,
Till your boys and girls were dead.

There is no marriage in Lidice,
There is no love or birth,
There is no drilling in the mines,
No ploughing of the earth.

But now we know your name, Lidice;
We see you from afar,
Not as a village lost in death
But as a guiding star.

Mazo de la Roche

With Only Five Plums:

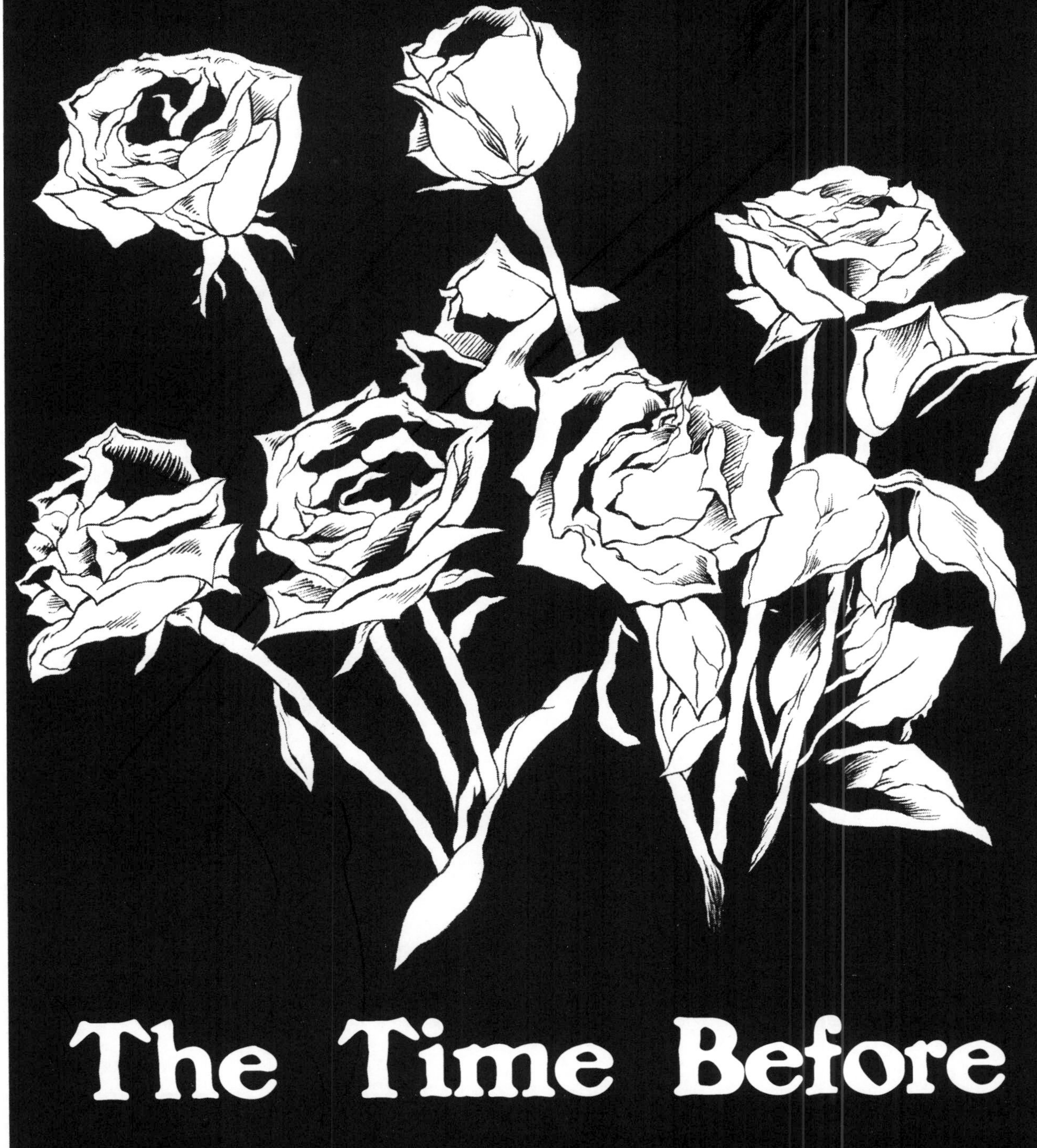

The Time Before

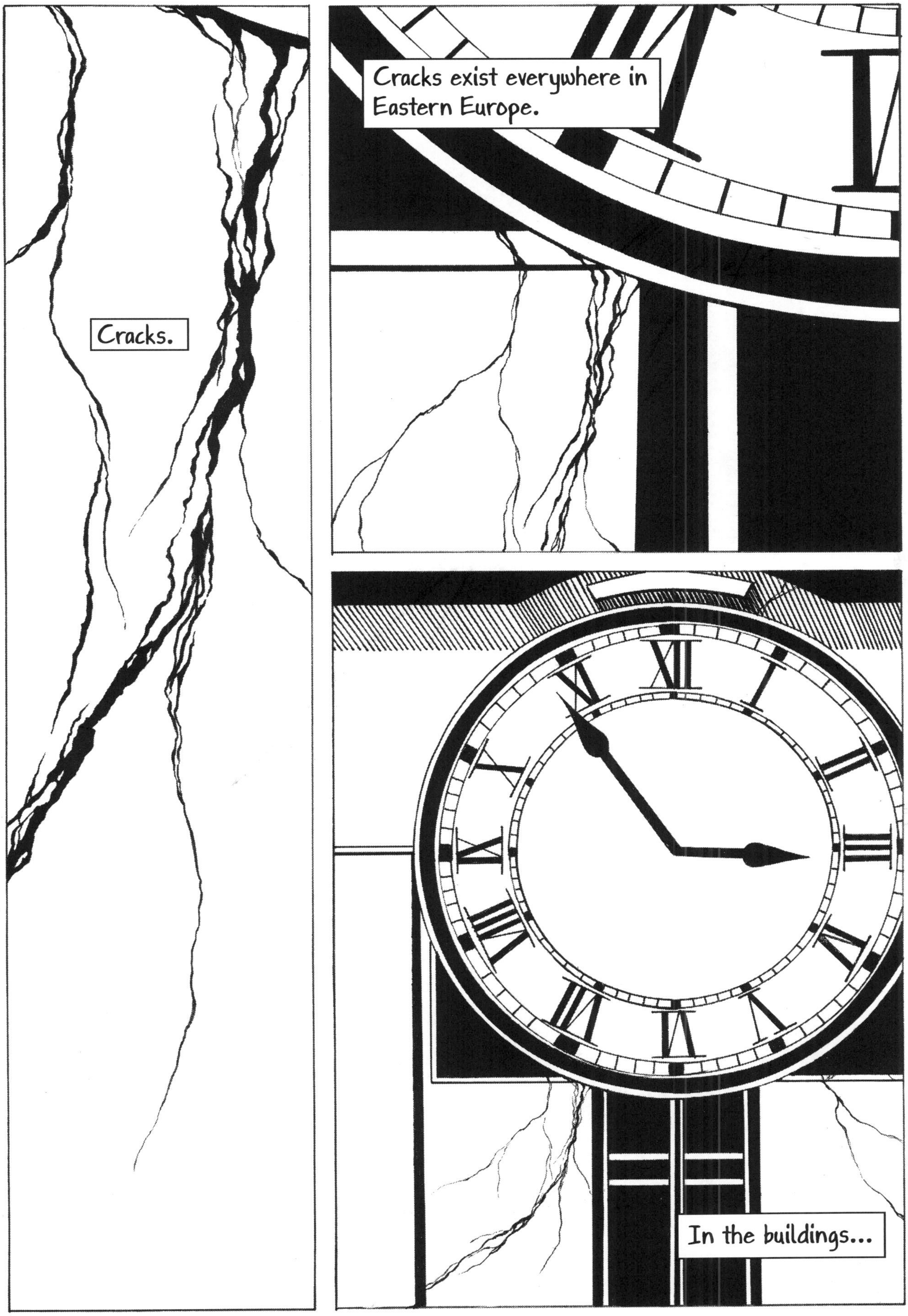
Cracks.
Cracks exist everywhere in Eastern Europe.
In the buildings...

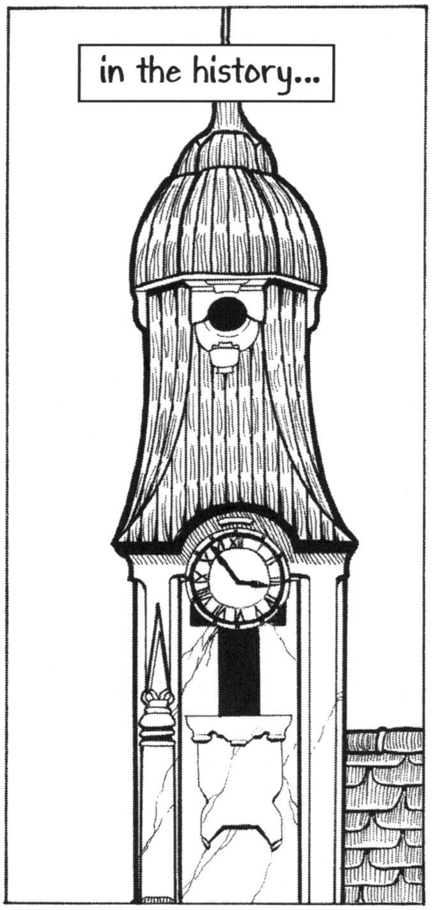
in the history...
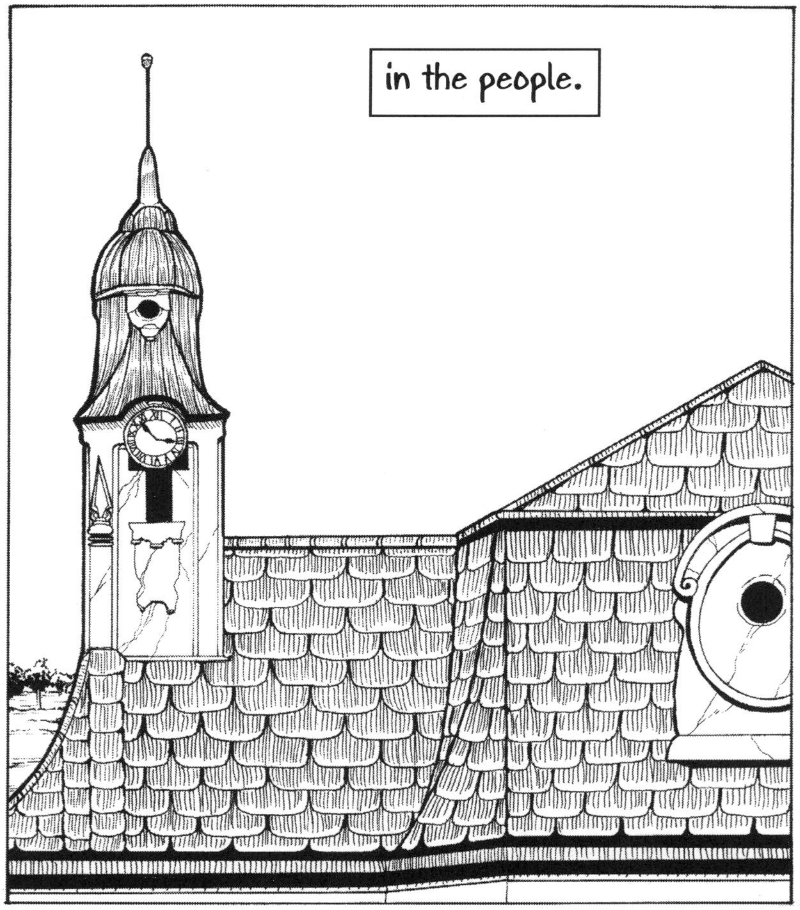
in the people.
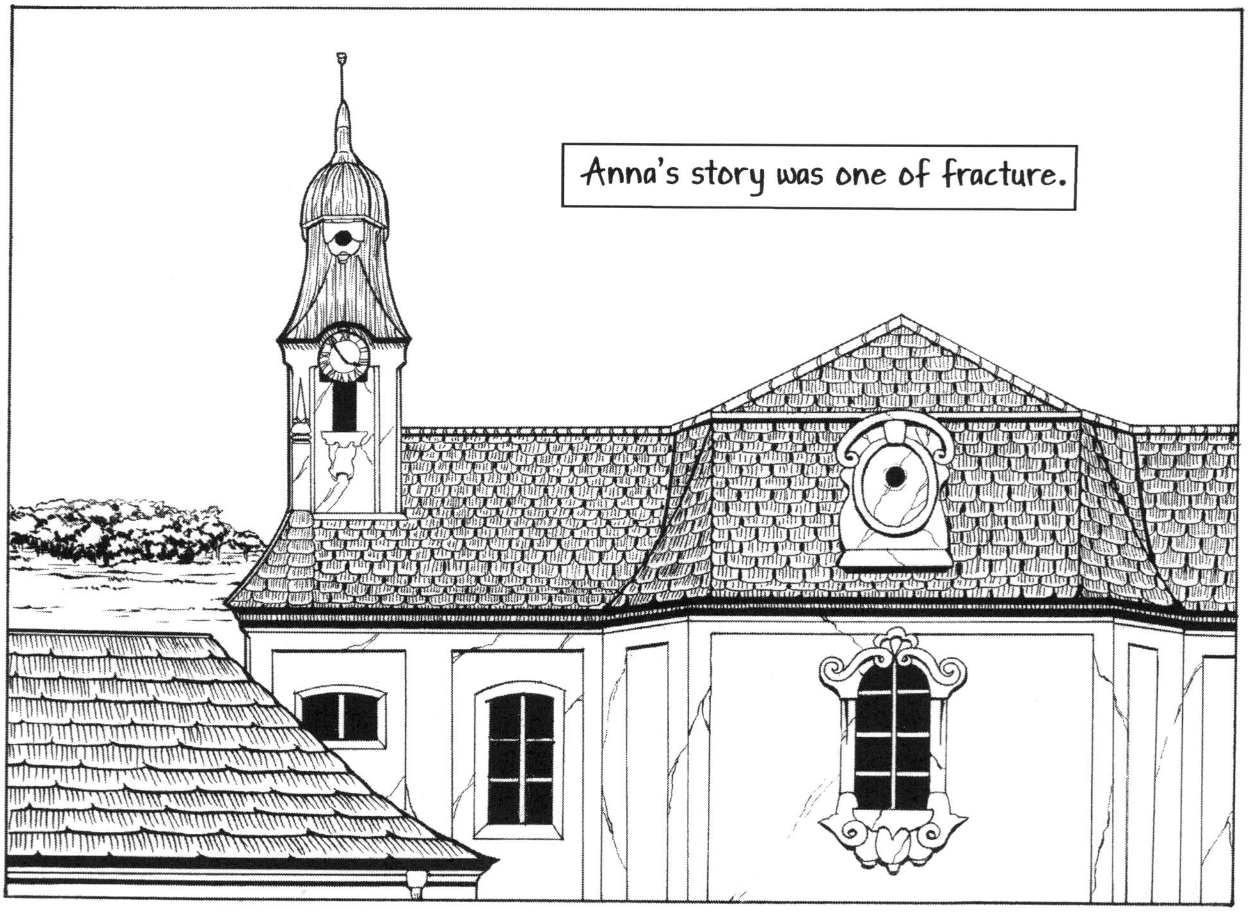
Anna's story was one of fracture.

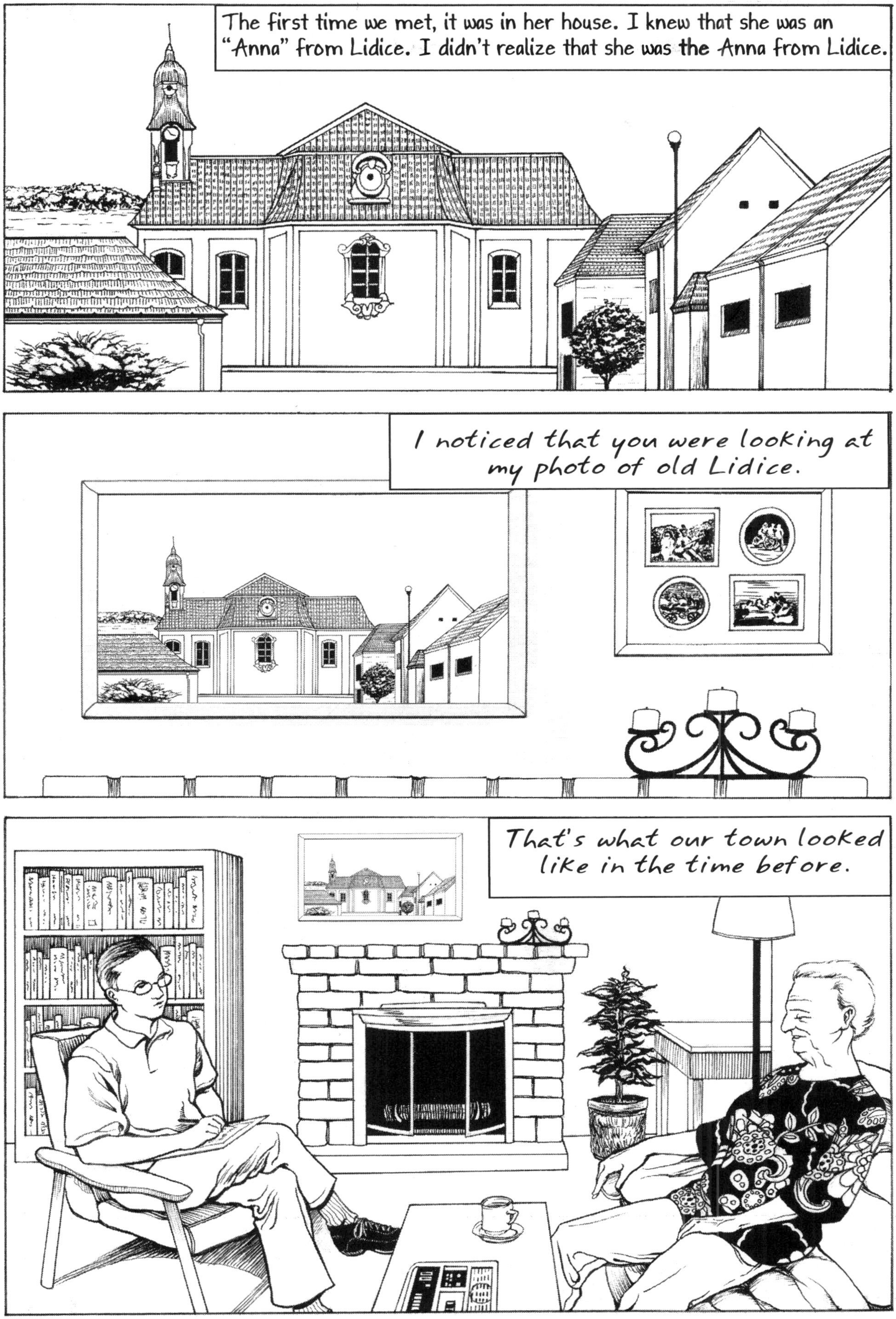
The first time we met, it was in her house. I knew that she was an "Anna" from Lidice. I didn't realize that she was the Anna from Lidice.
I noticed that you were looking at my photo of old Lidice.
That's what our town looked like in the time before.

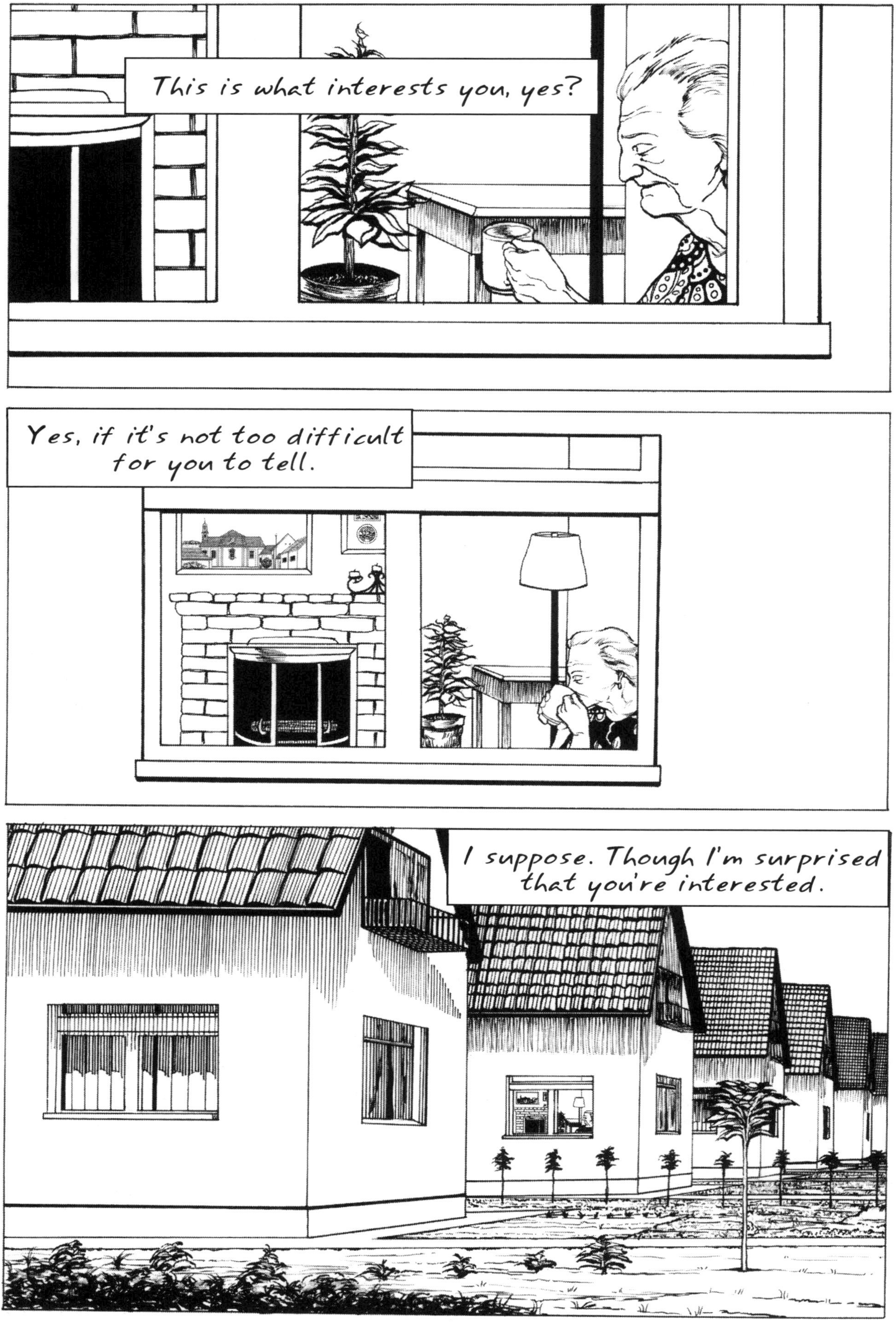
This is what interests you, yes?
Yes, if it's not too difficult for you to tell.
I suppose. Though I'm surprised that you're interested.

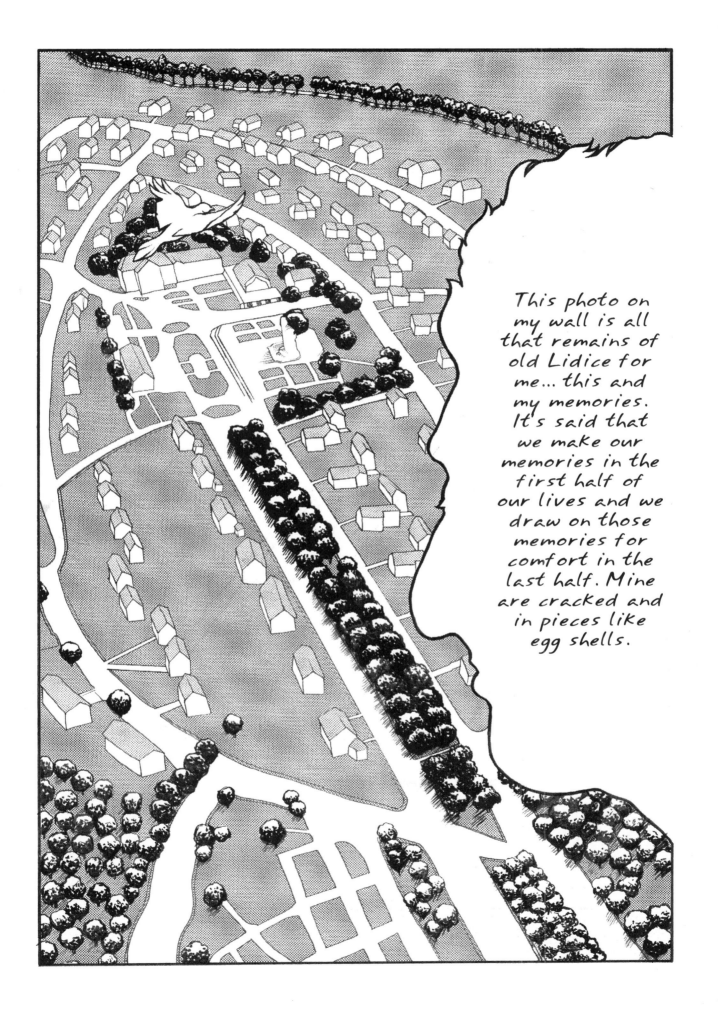

This photo on my wall is all that remains of old Lidice for me... this and my memories. It's said that we make our memories in the first half of our lives and we draw on those memories for comfort in the last half. Mine are cracked and in pieces like egg shells.

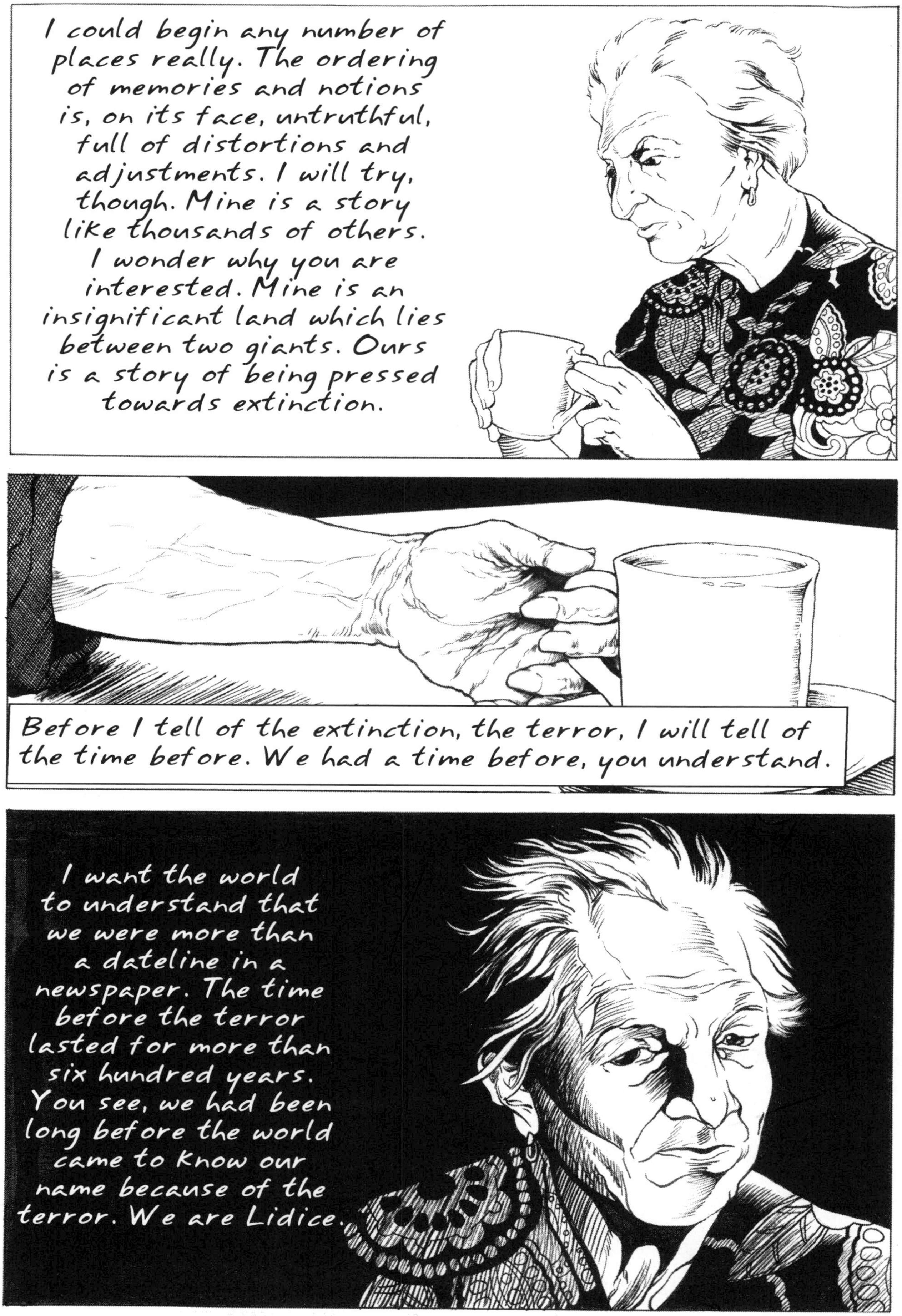

I could begin any number of places really. The ordering of memories and notions is, on its face, untruthful, full of distortions and adjustments. I will try, though. Mine is a story like thousands of others. I wonder why you are interested. Mine is an insignificant land which lies between two giants. Ours is a story of being pressed towards extinction.

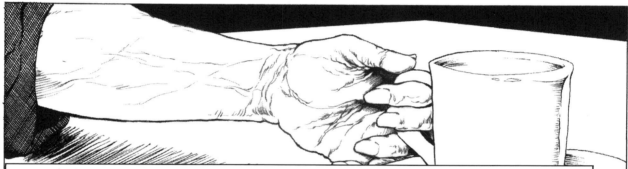

Before I tell of the extinction, the terror, I will tell of the time before. We had a time before, you understand.

I want the world to understand that we were more than a dateline in a newspaper. The time before the terror lasted for more than six hundred years. You see, we had been long before the world came to know our name because of the terror. We are Lidice.

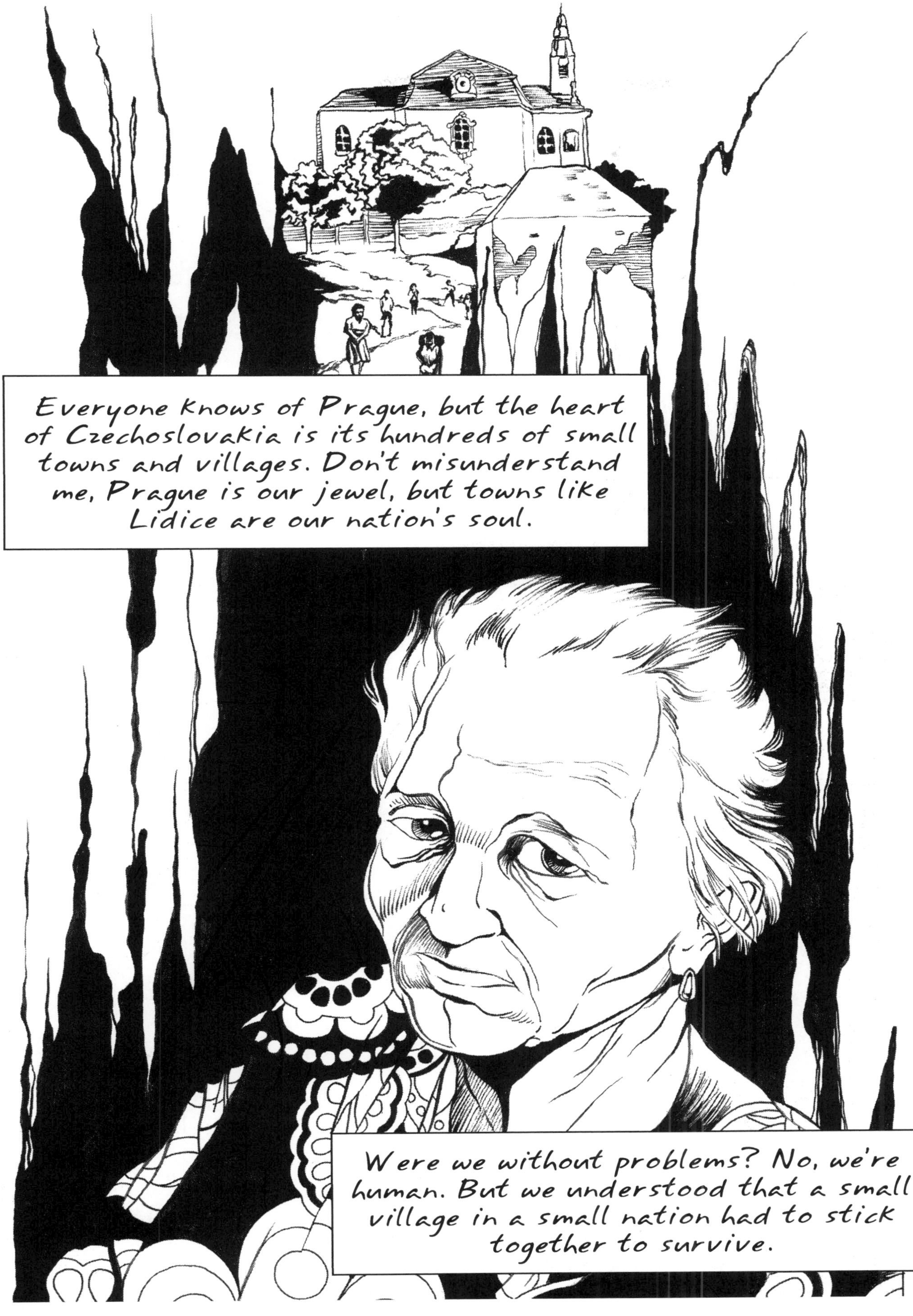
Everyone knows of Prague, but the heart of Czechoslovakia is its hundreds of small towns and villages. Don't misunderstand me, Prague is our jewel, but towns like Lidice are our nation's soul.
Were we without problems? No, we're human. But we understood that a small village in a small nation had to stick together to survive.

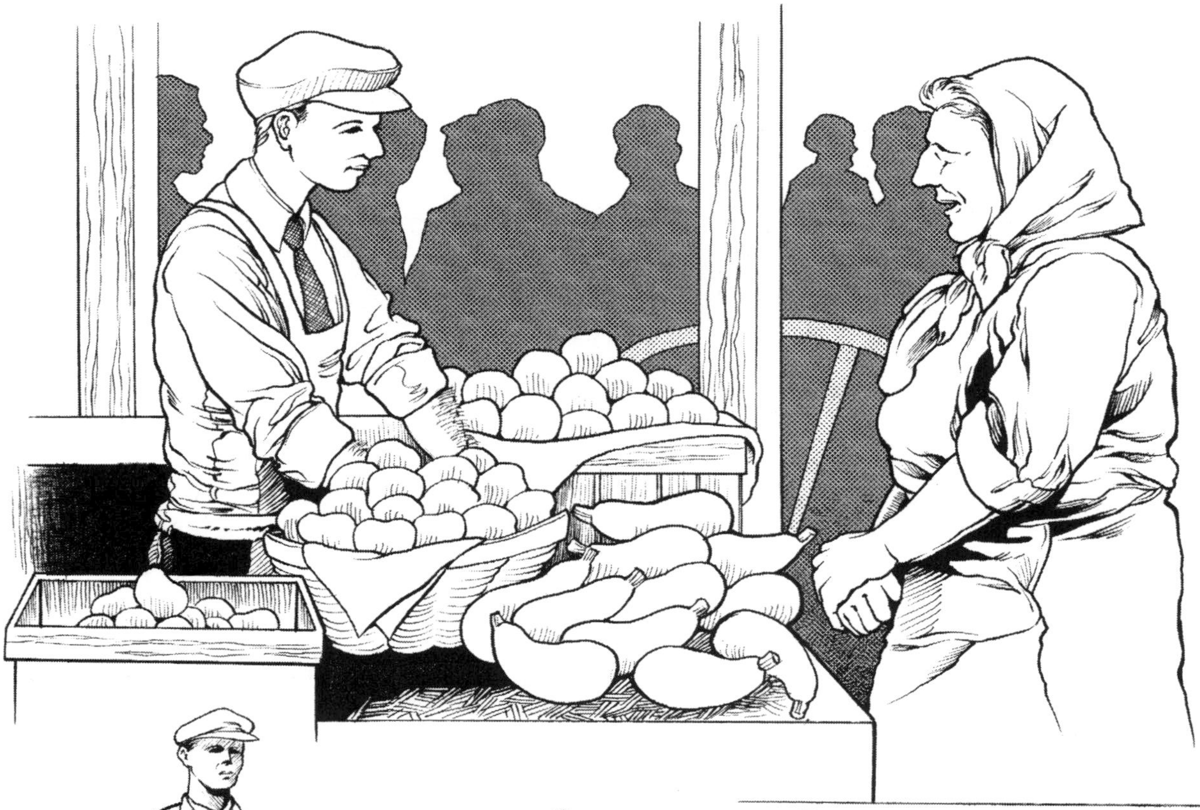

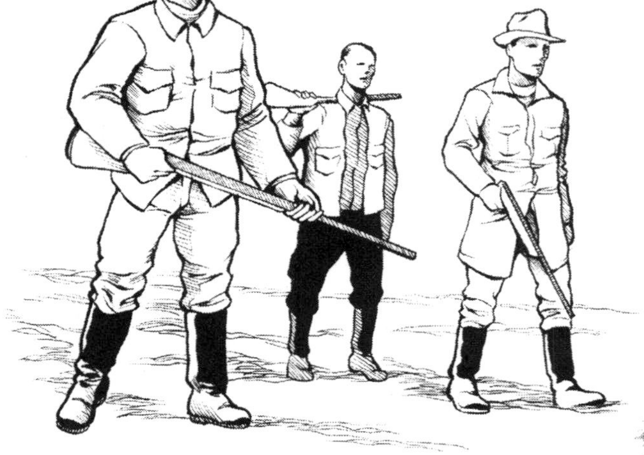

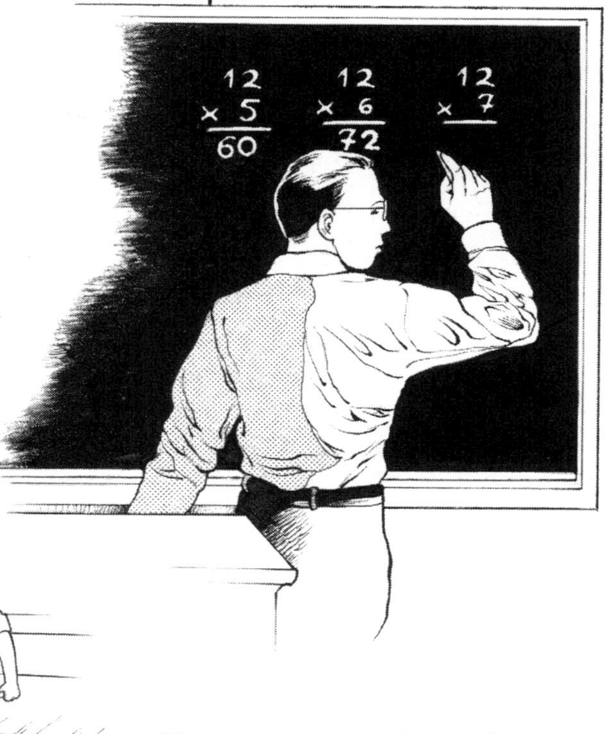
12
× 5
60
12
× 6
72
12
× 7

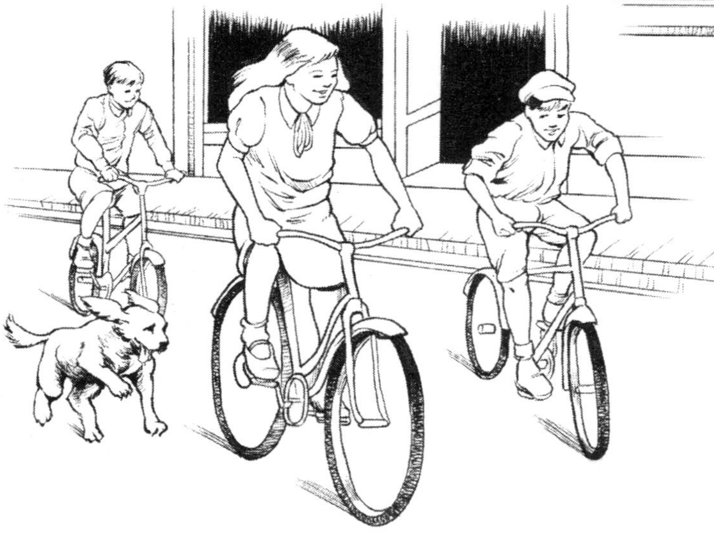

From our village's first
breath in the morning,
there was life in its
narrow streets.

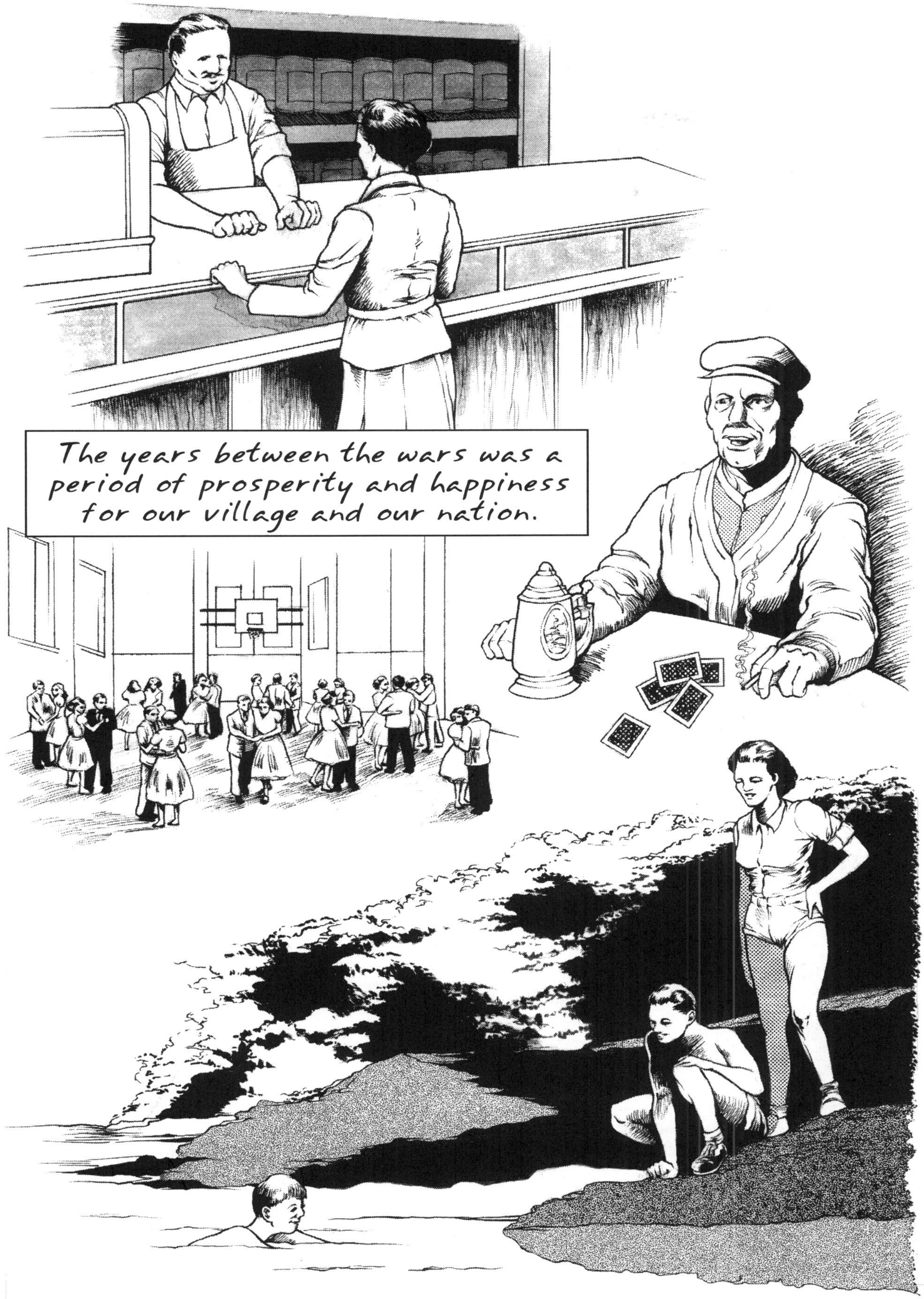
The years between the wars was a period of prosperity and happiness for our village and our nation.

We knew these good times weren't likely to last forever. We've come to expect troubles from our neighbors. History bears that out in our part of the world.

There was genuine friendship among the villagers.

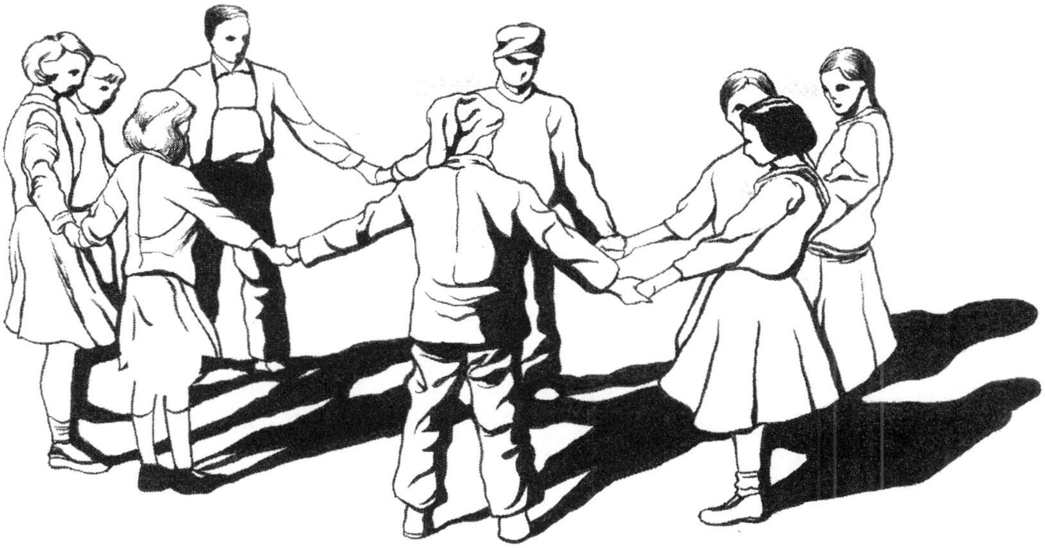

Whether it was among our children in school...

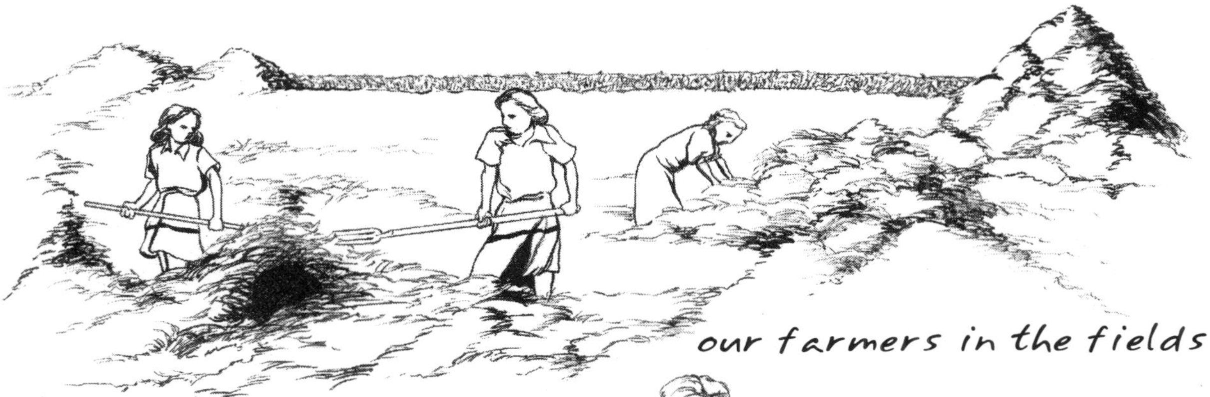
our farmers in the fields...

our workers in the foundry...

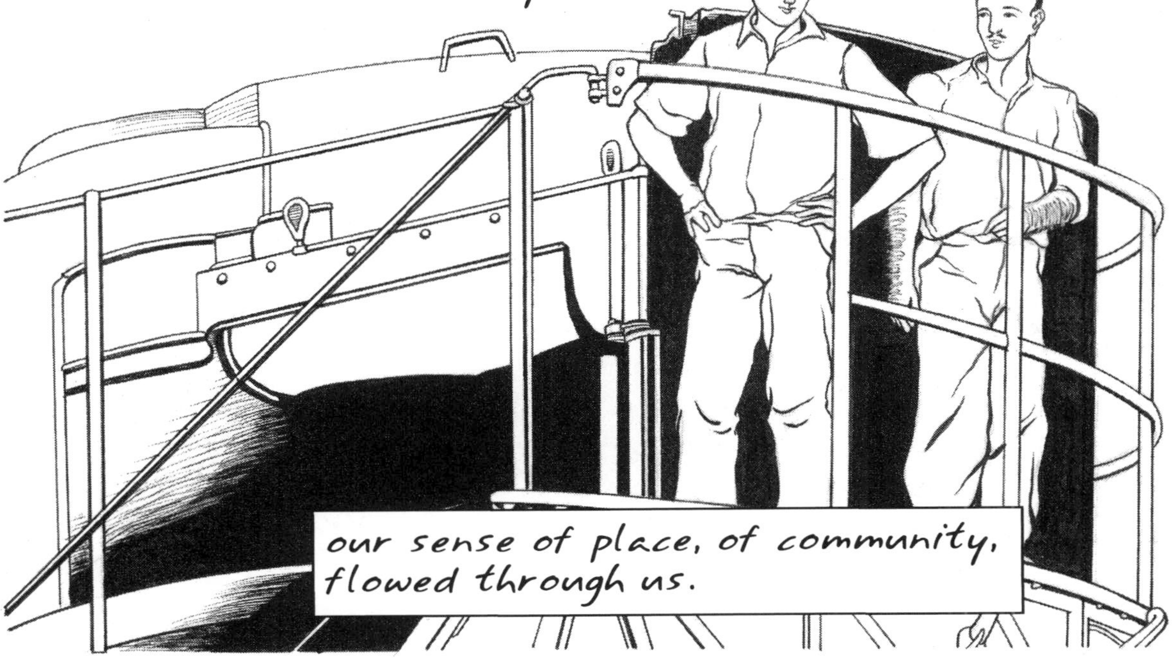
our sense of place, of community,
flowed through us.

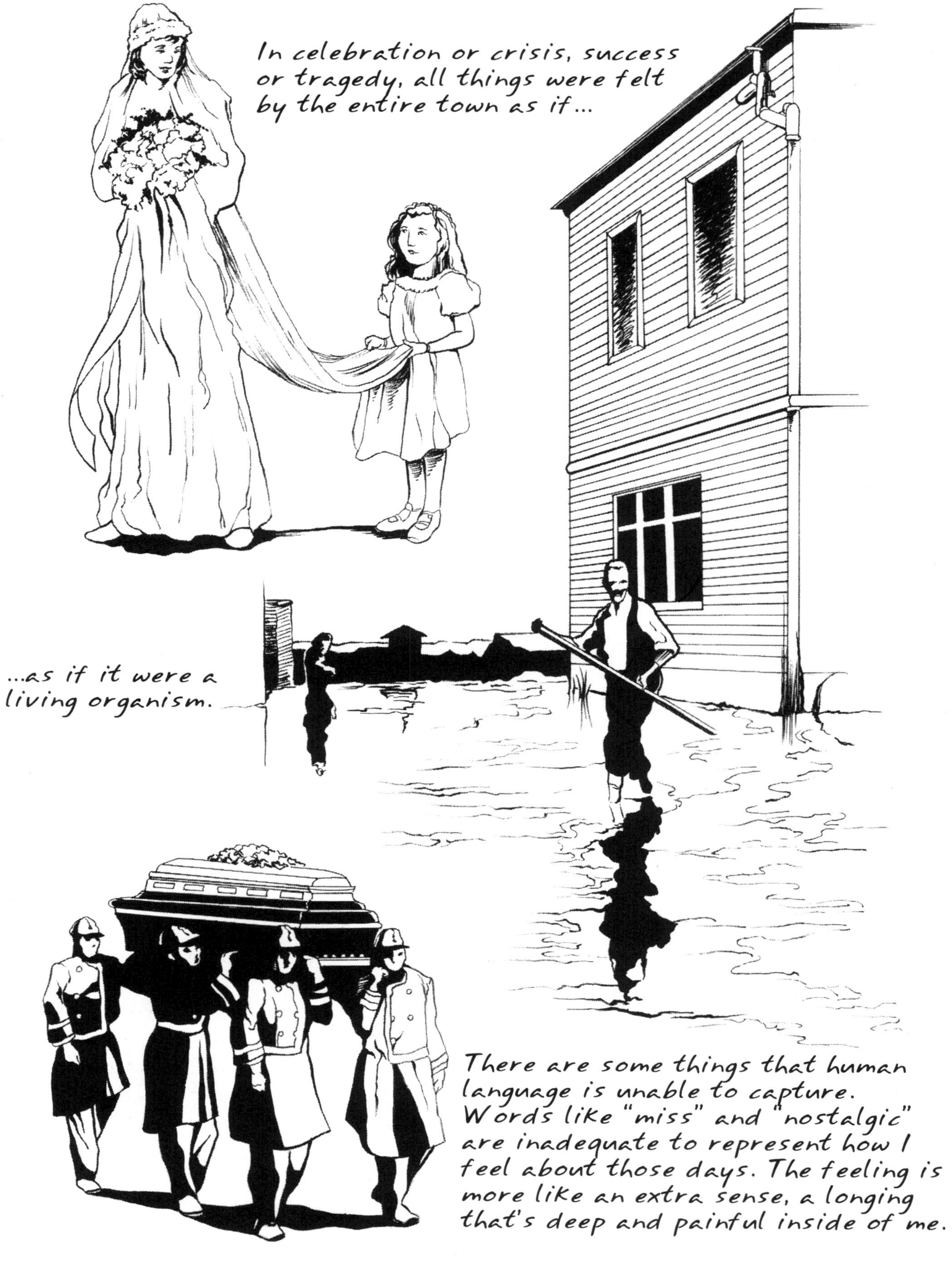
In celebration or crisis, success or tragedy, all things were felt by the entire town as if...
...as if it were a living organism.
There are some things that human language is unable to capture. Words like "miss" and "nostalgic" are inadequate to represent how I feel about those days. The feeling is more like an extra sense, a longing that's deep and painful inside of me.

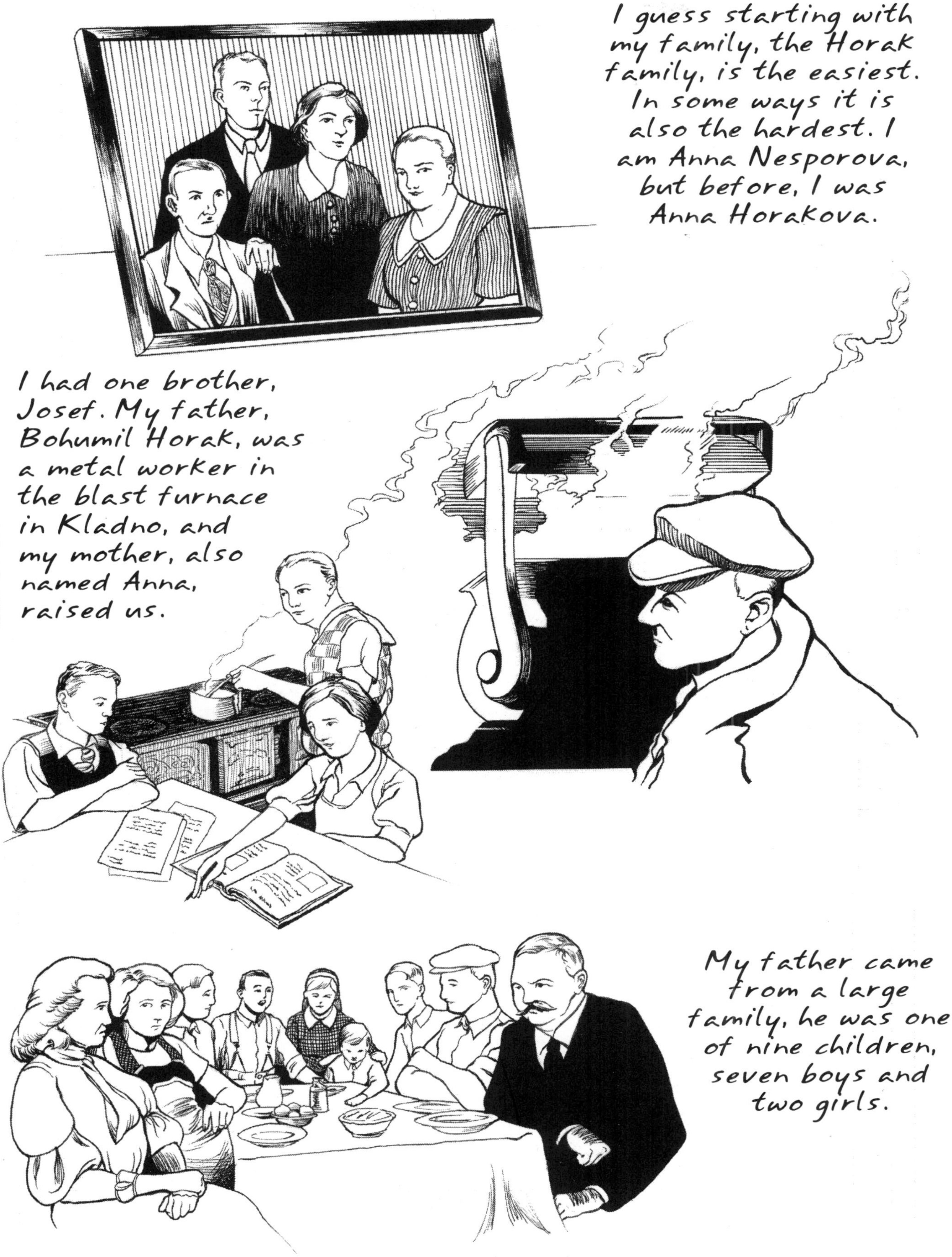
I guess starting with my family, the Horak family, is the easiest. In some ways it is also the hardest. I am Anna Nesporova, but before, I was Anna Horakova.
I had one brother, Josef. My father, Bohumil Horak, was a metal worker in the blast furnace in Kladno, and my mother, also named Anna, raised us.
My father came from a large family, he was one of nine children, seven boys and two girls.

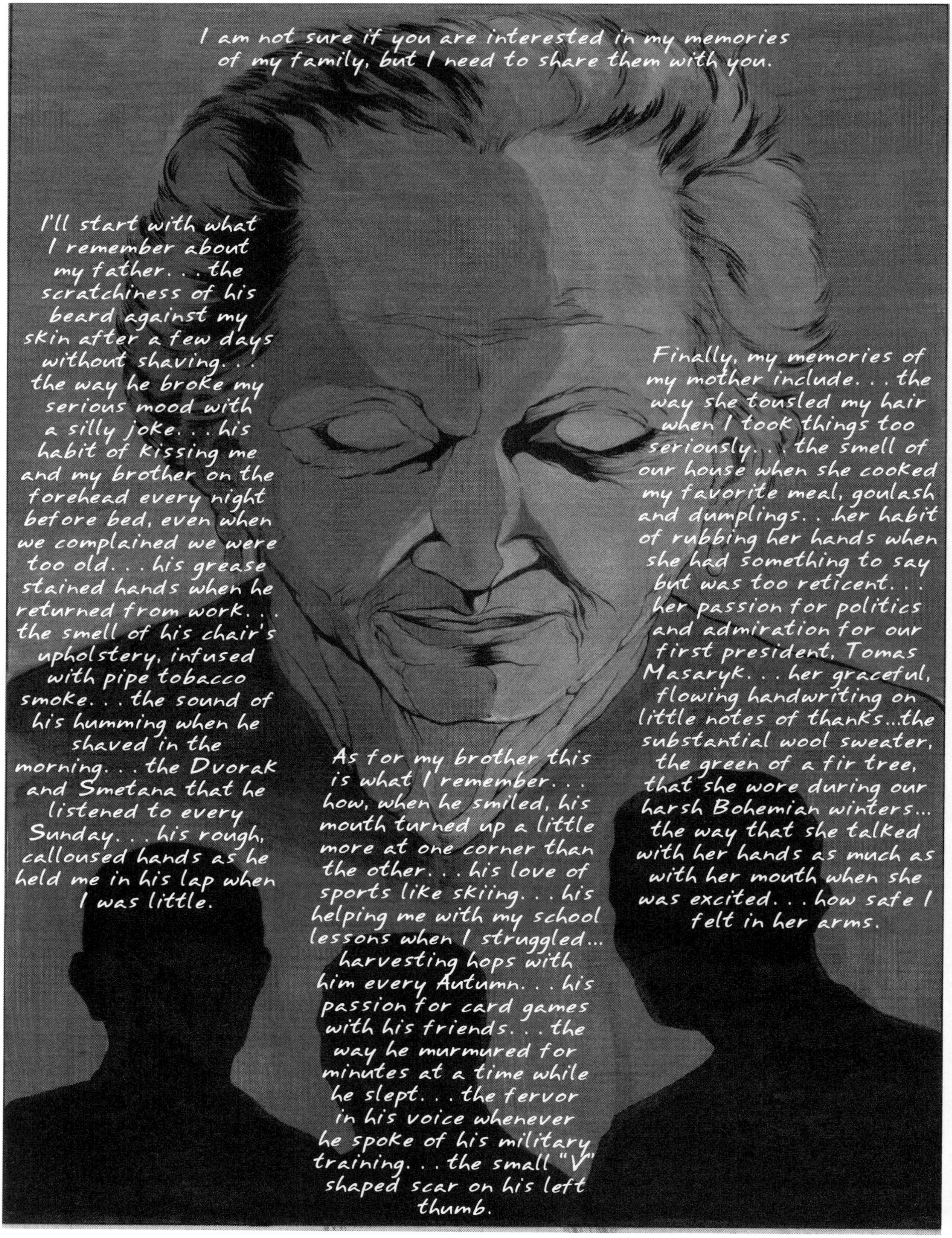
I am not sure if you are interested in my memories of my family, but I need to share them with you.
I'll start with what I remember about my father. . . the scratchiness of his beard against my skin after a few days without shaving. . . the way he broke my serious mood with a silly joke. . . his habit of kissing me and my brother on the forehead every night before bed, even when we complained we were too old. . . his grease stained hands when he returned from work. . . the smell of his chair's upholstery, infused with pipe tobacco smoke. . . the sound of his humming when he shaved in the morning. . . the Dvorak and Smetana that he listened to every Sunday. . . his rough, calloused hands as he held me in his lap when I was little.
As for my brother this is what I remember. . . how, when he smiled, his mouth turned up a little more at one corner than the other. . . his love of sports like skiing. . . his helping me with my school lessons when I struggled... harvesting hops with him every Autumn. . . his passion for card games with his friends. . . the way he murmured for minutes at a time while he slept. . . the fervor in his voice whenever he spoke of his military training. . . the small "V" shaped scar on his left thumb.
Finally, my memories of my mother include. . . the way she tousled my hair when I took things too seriously. . . the smell of our house when she cooked my favorite meal, goulash and dumplings. . .her habit of rubbing her hands when she had something to say but was too reticent. . . her passion for politics and admiration for our first president, Tomas Masaryk. . . her graceful, flowing handwriting on little notes of thanks...the substantial wool sweater, the green of a fir tree, that she wore during our harsh Bohemian winters... the way that she talked with her hands as much as with her mouth when she was excited. . . how safe I felt in her arms.

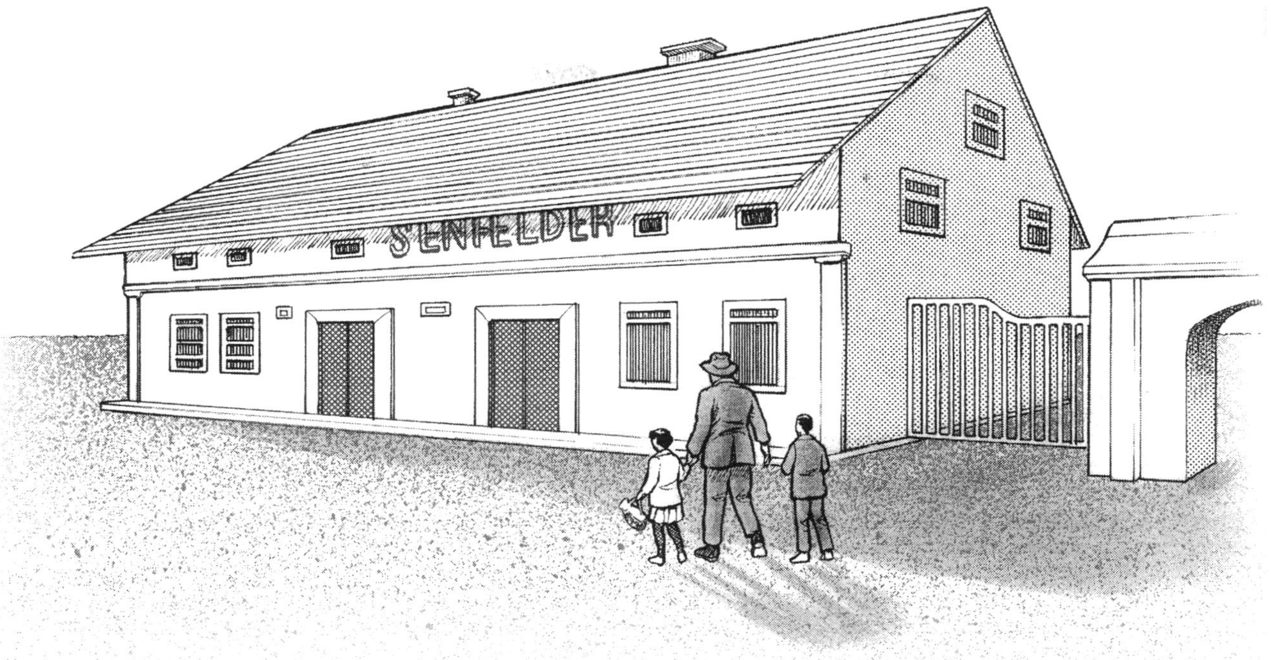
SENFELDER

I remember when I was a little girl, my father used to take me and my brother to Senfelder's pub almost every Saturday evening. We always went before our family's big Saturday supper to fill our pitcher with beer.

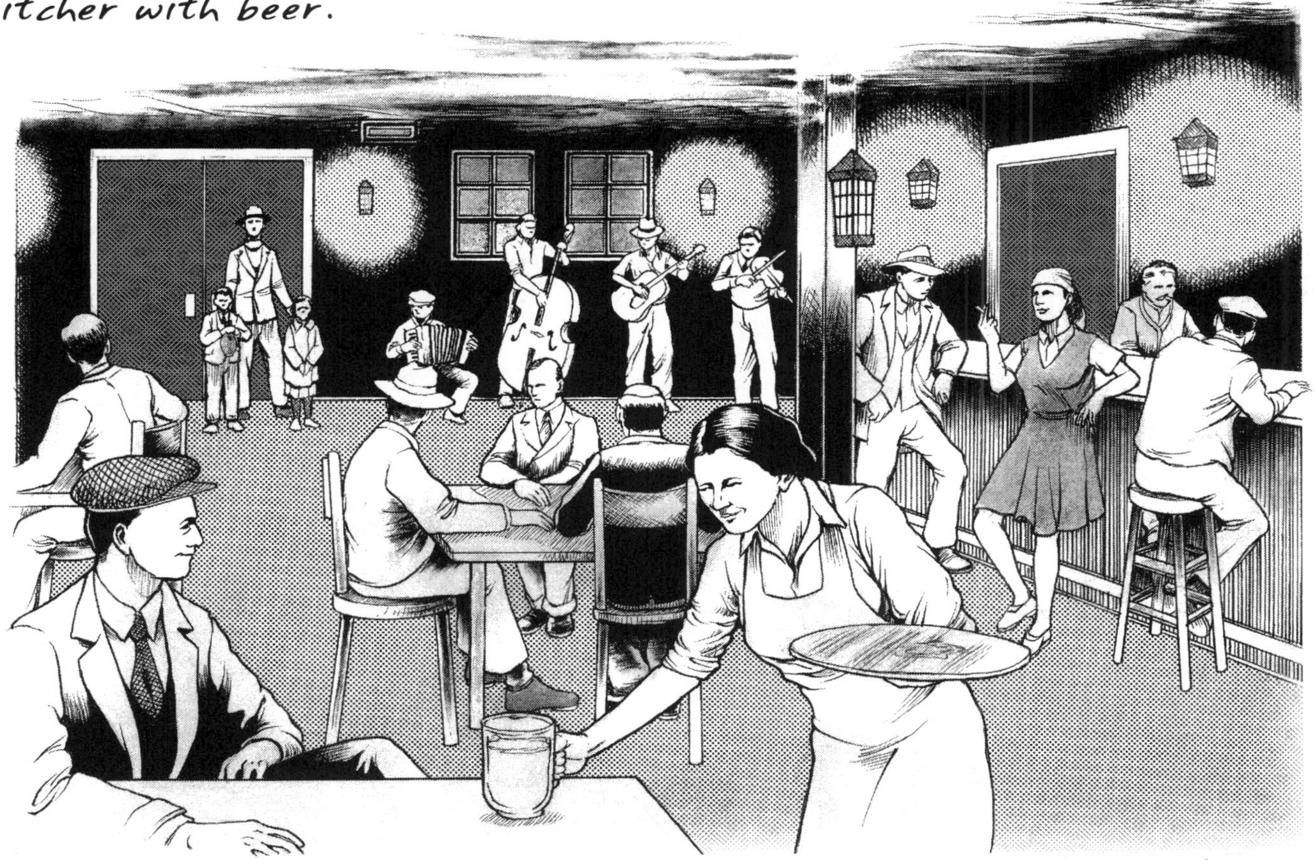

I loved our Saturday trips to the pub. They brought me into a world of sights, sounds, and smells that I rarely experienced elsewhere. The food and the music. The laughter and the smoke. They were curious and thrilling to me.

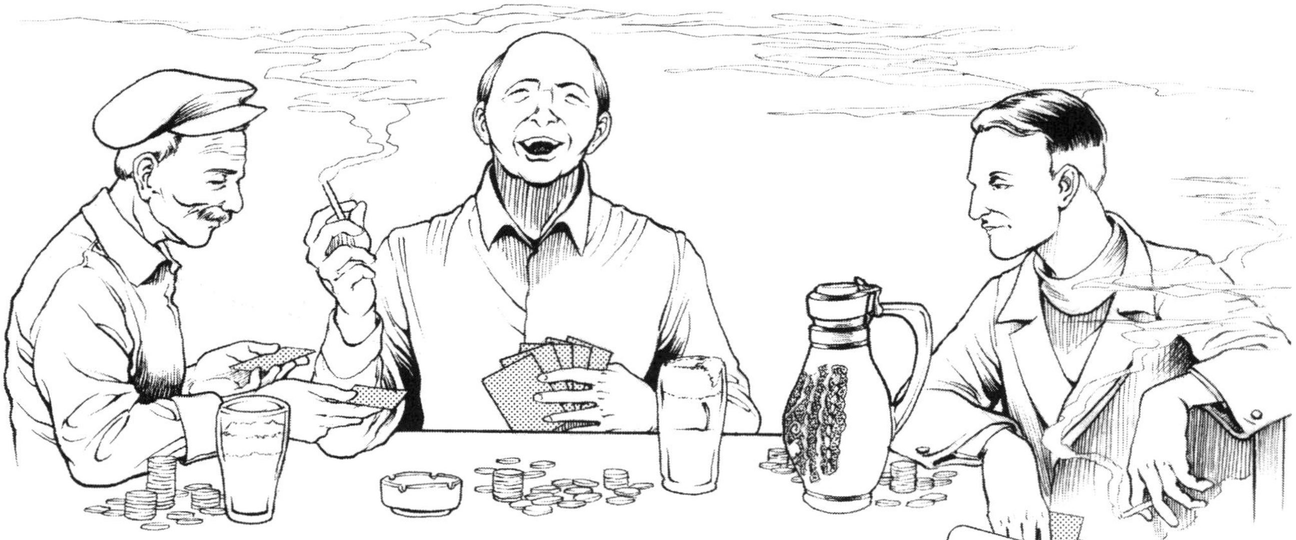

My father always stayed to play a game of Marias, our favorite card game, with his friends.

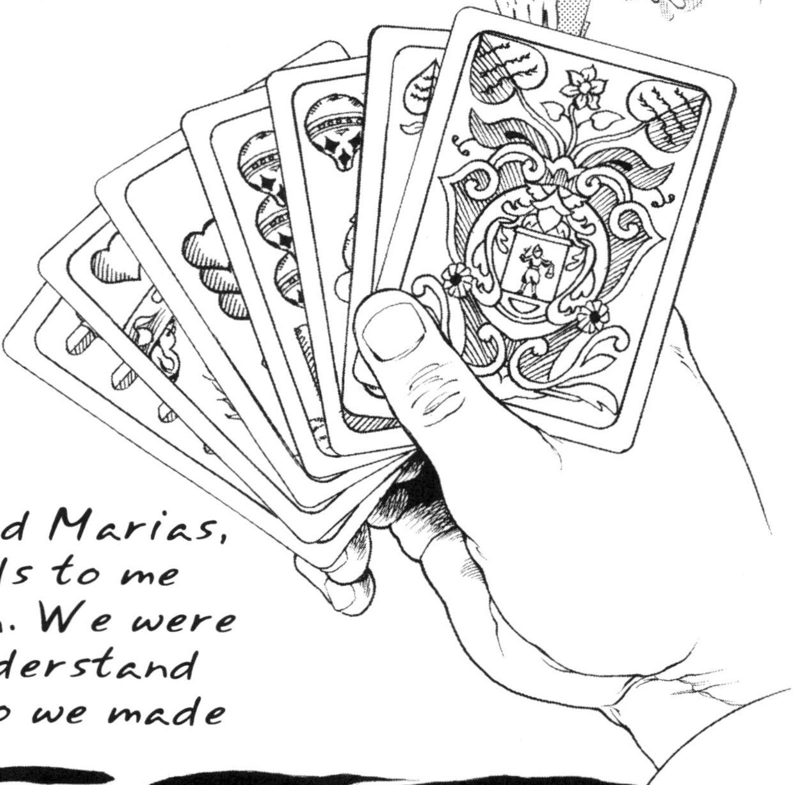

While my father played Marias, he gave a deck of cards to me and Josef to play with. We were too young to really understand the rules of Marias, so we made up our own games.

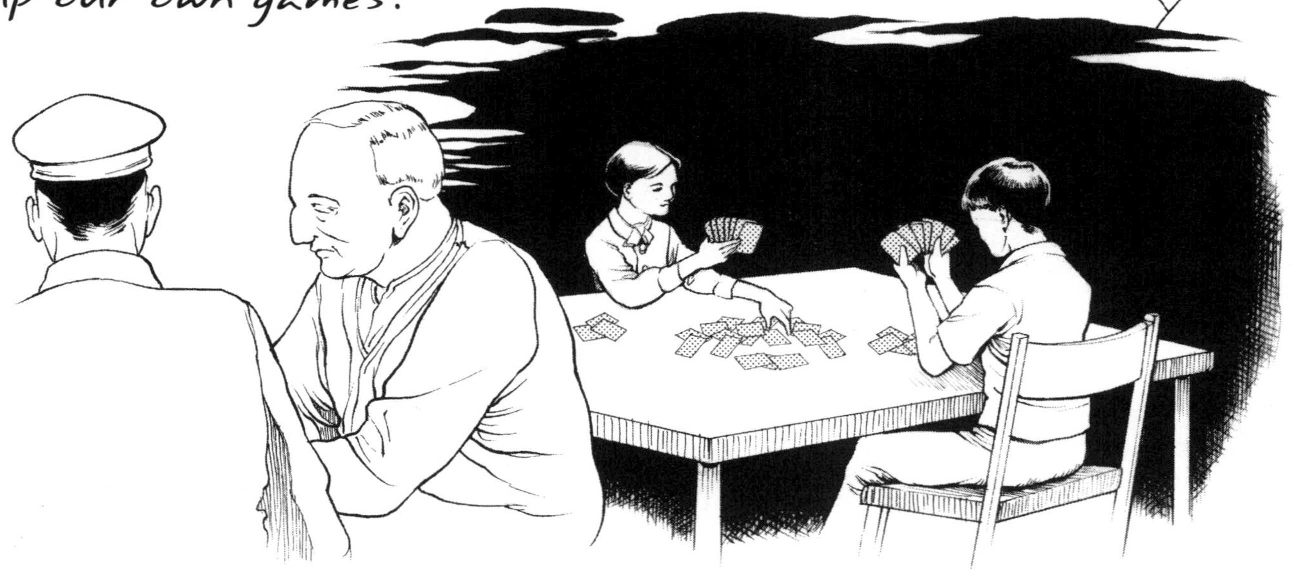

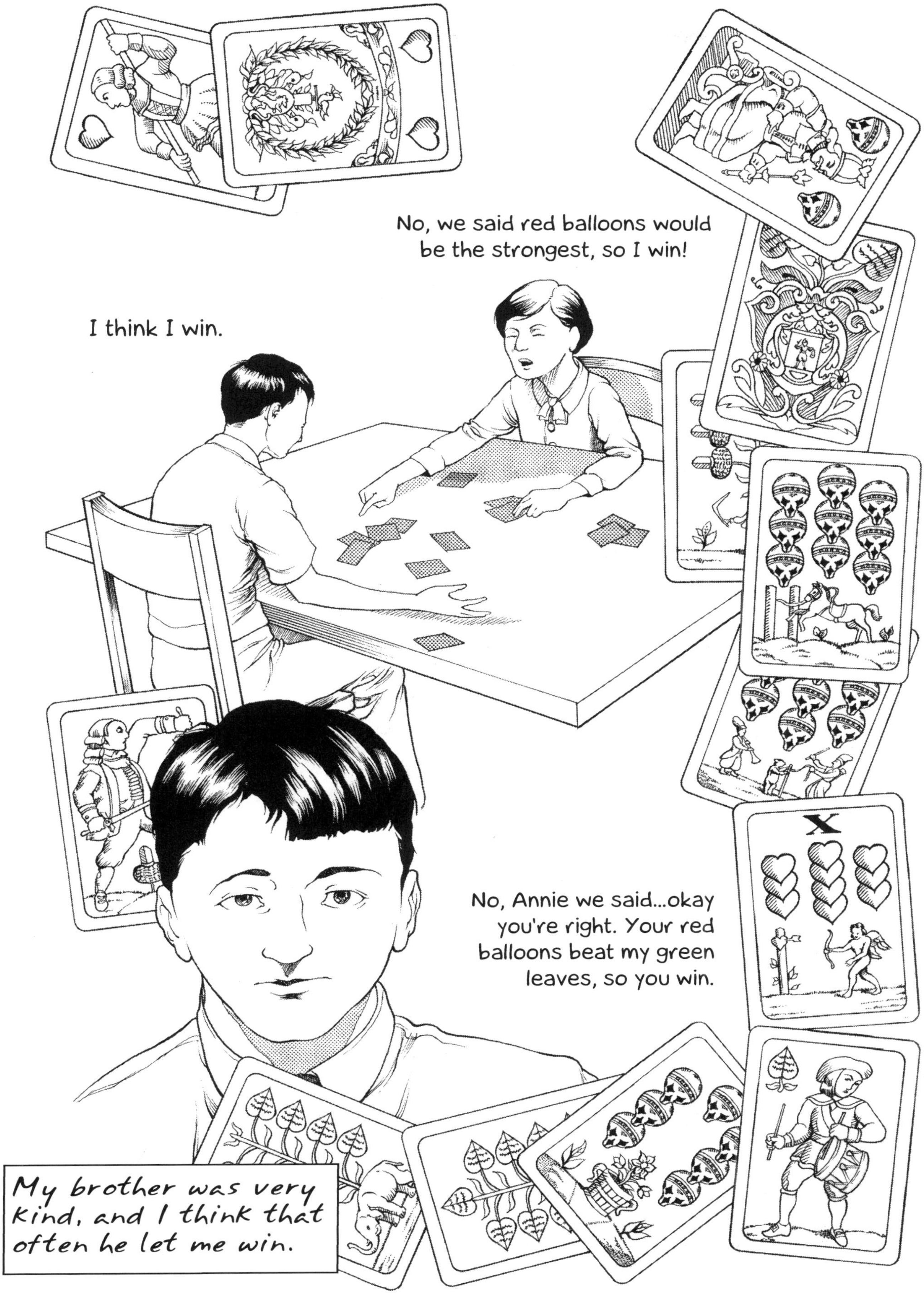
I think I win.
No, we said red balloons would be the strongest, so I win!
No, Annie we said...okay you're right. Your red balloons beat my green leaves, so you win.
X
My brother was very kind, and I think that often he let me win.

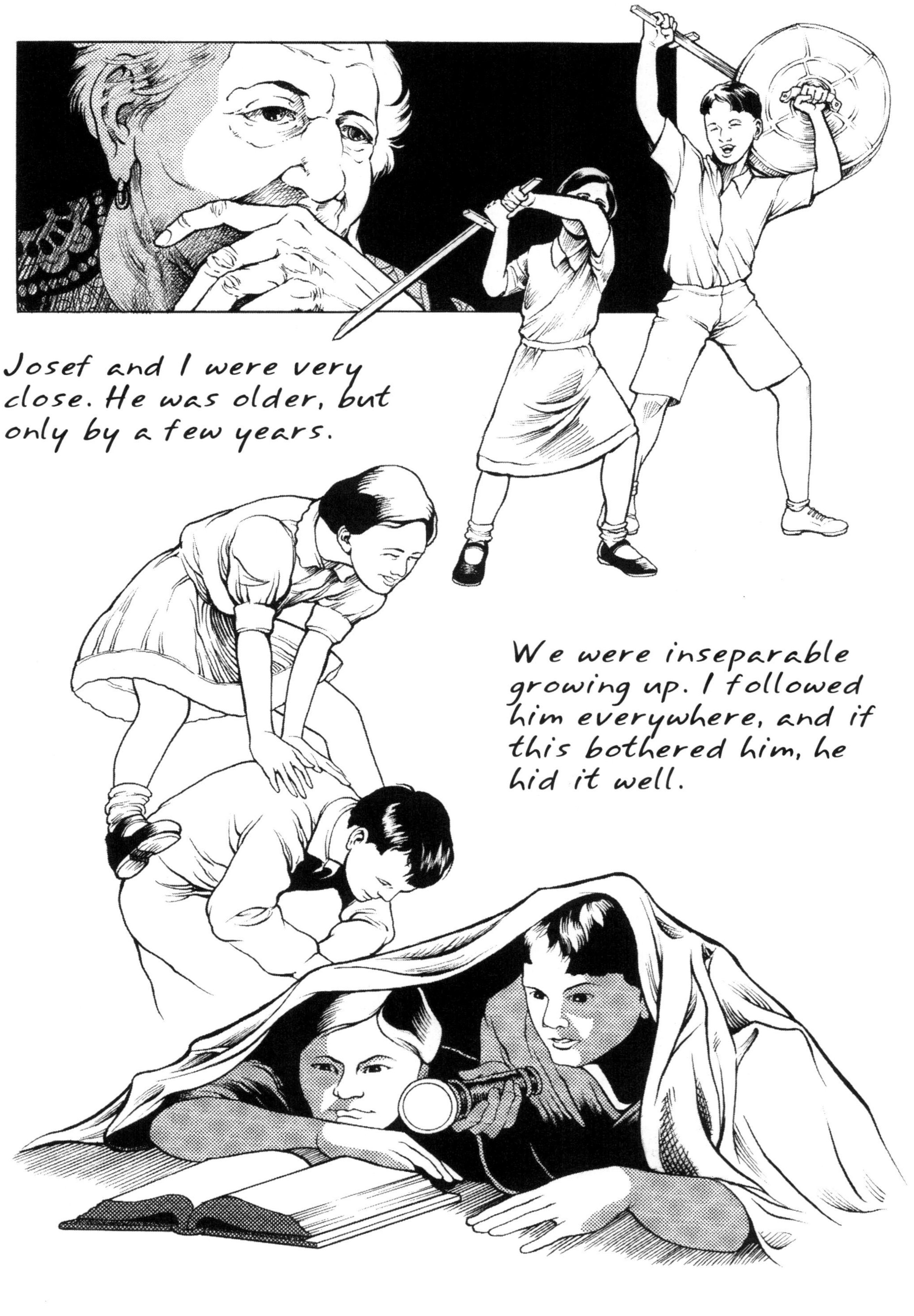
Josef and I were very close. He was older, but only by a few years.
We were inseparable growing up. I followed him everywhere, and if this bothered him, he hid it well.

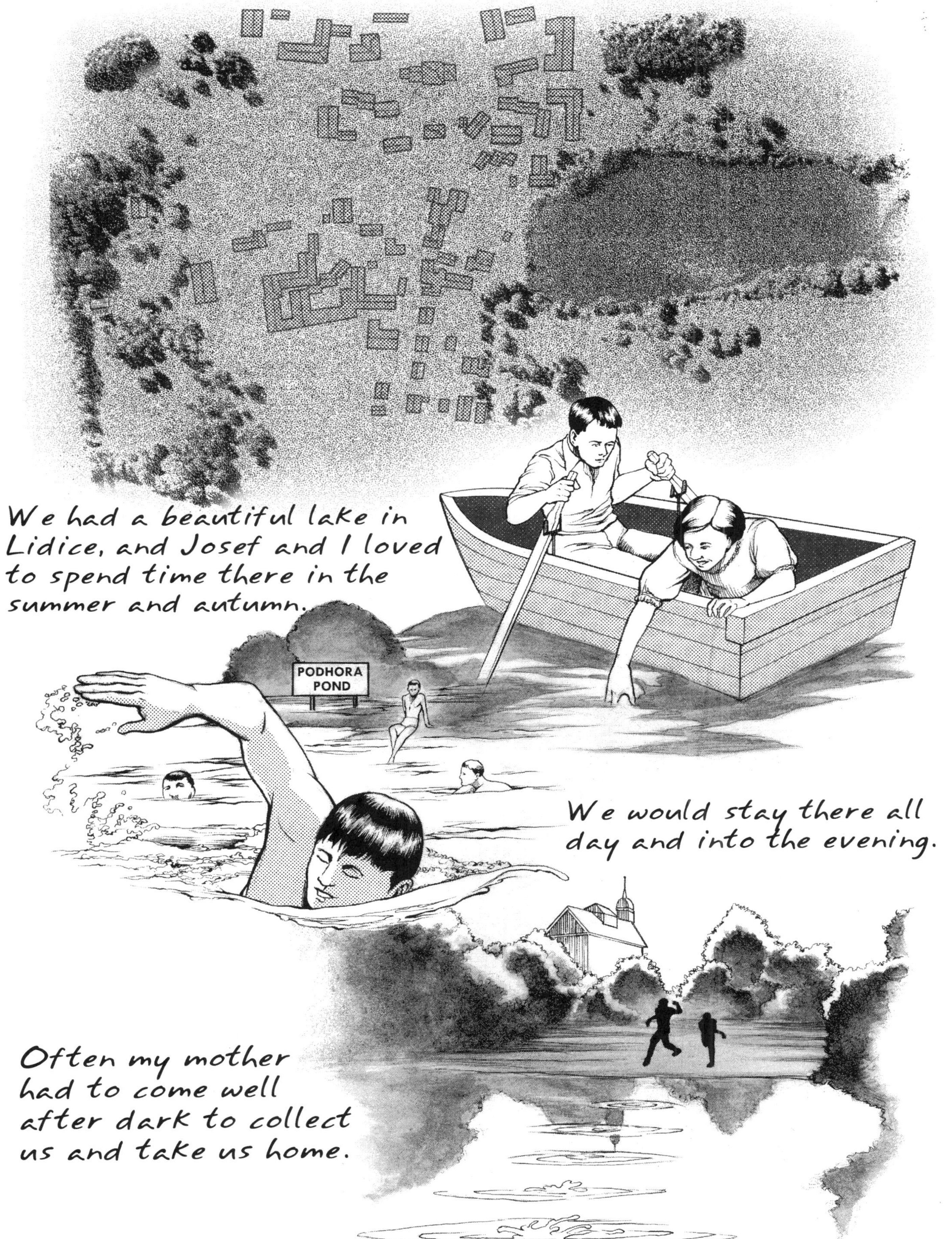
We had a beautiful lake in Lidice, and Josef and I loved to spend time there in the summer and autumn.
PODHORA POND
We would stay there all day and into the evening.
Often my mother had to come well after dark to collect us and take us home.

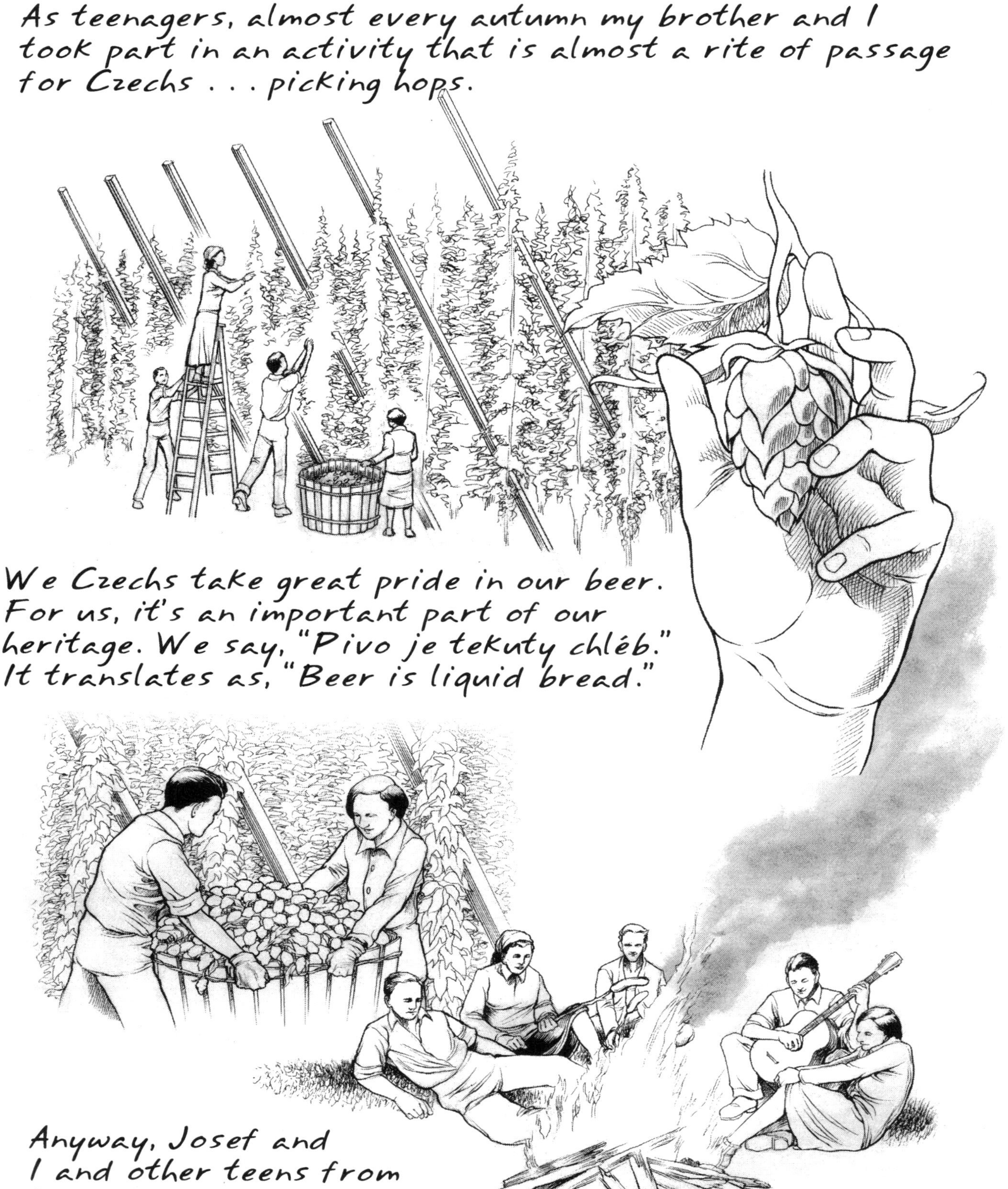
As teenagers, almost every autumn my brother and I took part in an activity that is almost a rite of passage for Czechs . . . picking hops.
We Czechs take great pride in our beer. For us, it's an important part of our heritage. We say, "Pivo je tekuty chléb." It translates as, "Beer is liquid bread."
Anyway, Josef and I and other teens from Lidice spent many autumns caravanning around Bohemia harvesting hops. Some of my fondest memories of Josef are from this time.

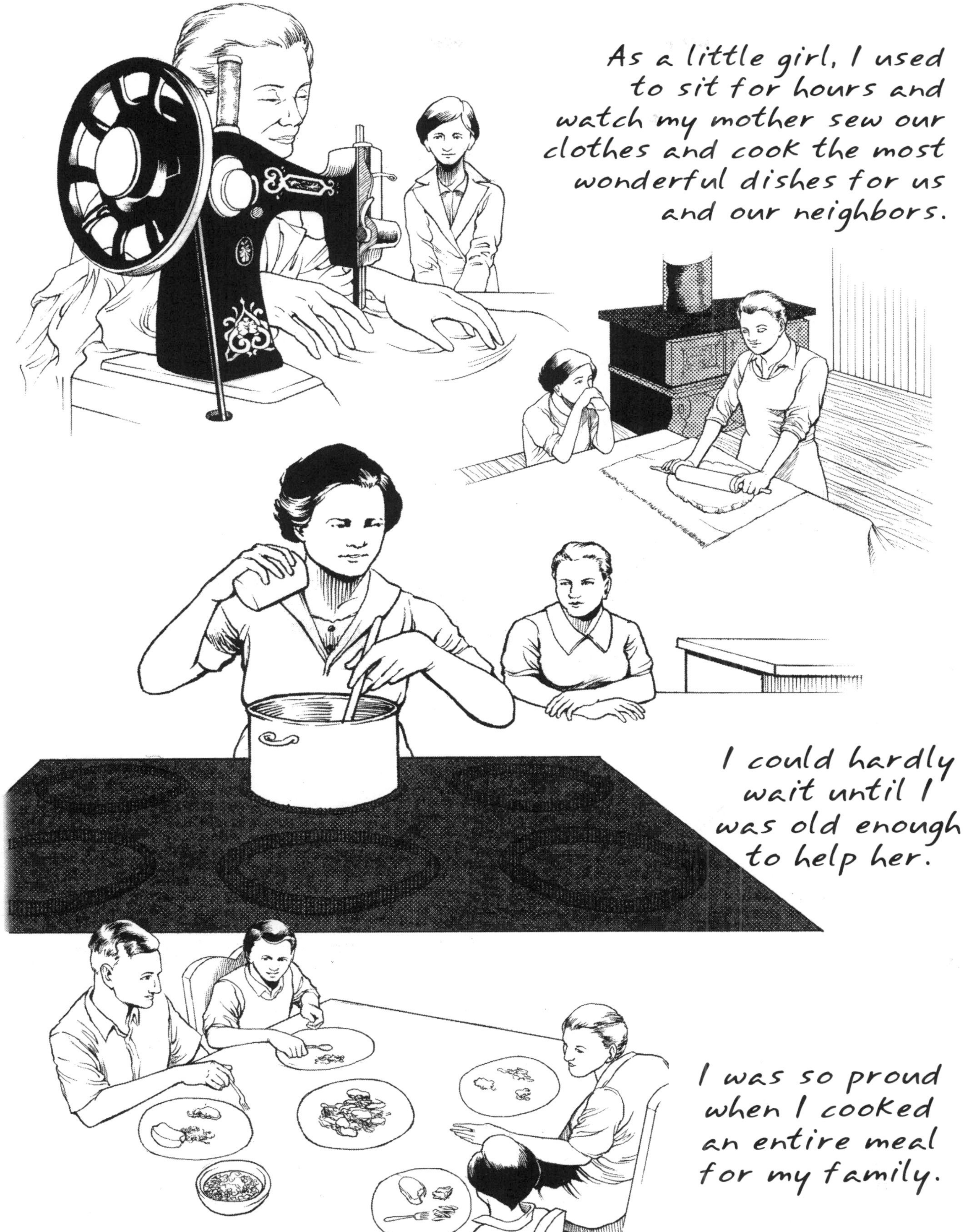
As a little girl, I used to sit for hours and watch my mother sew our clothes and cook the most wonderful dishes for us and our neighbors.
I could hardly wait until I was old enough to help her.
I was so proud when I cooked an entire meal for my family.

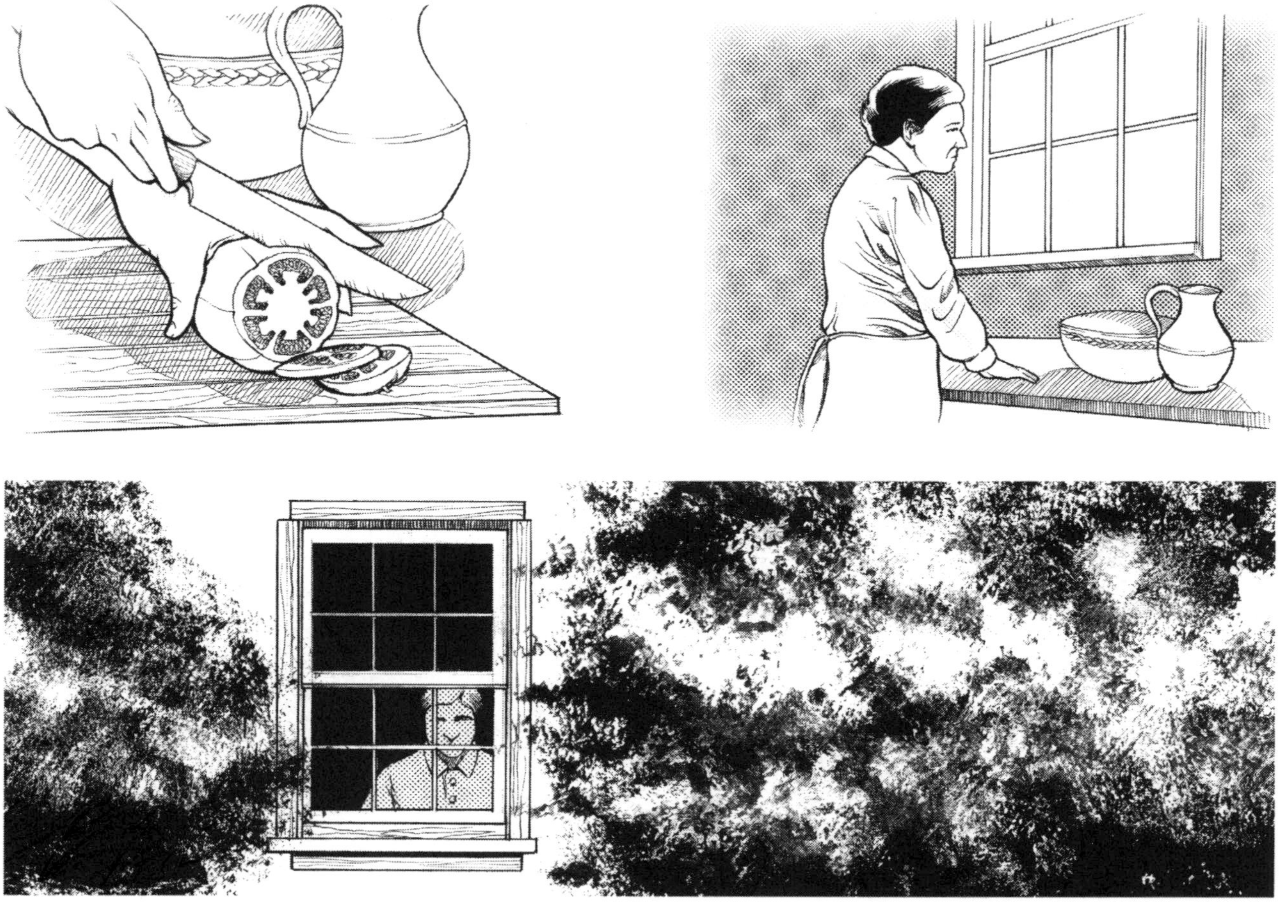

I still make some of her recipes today.

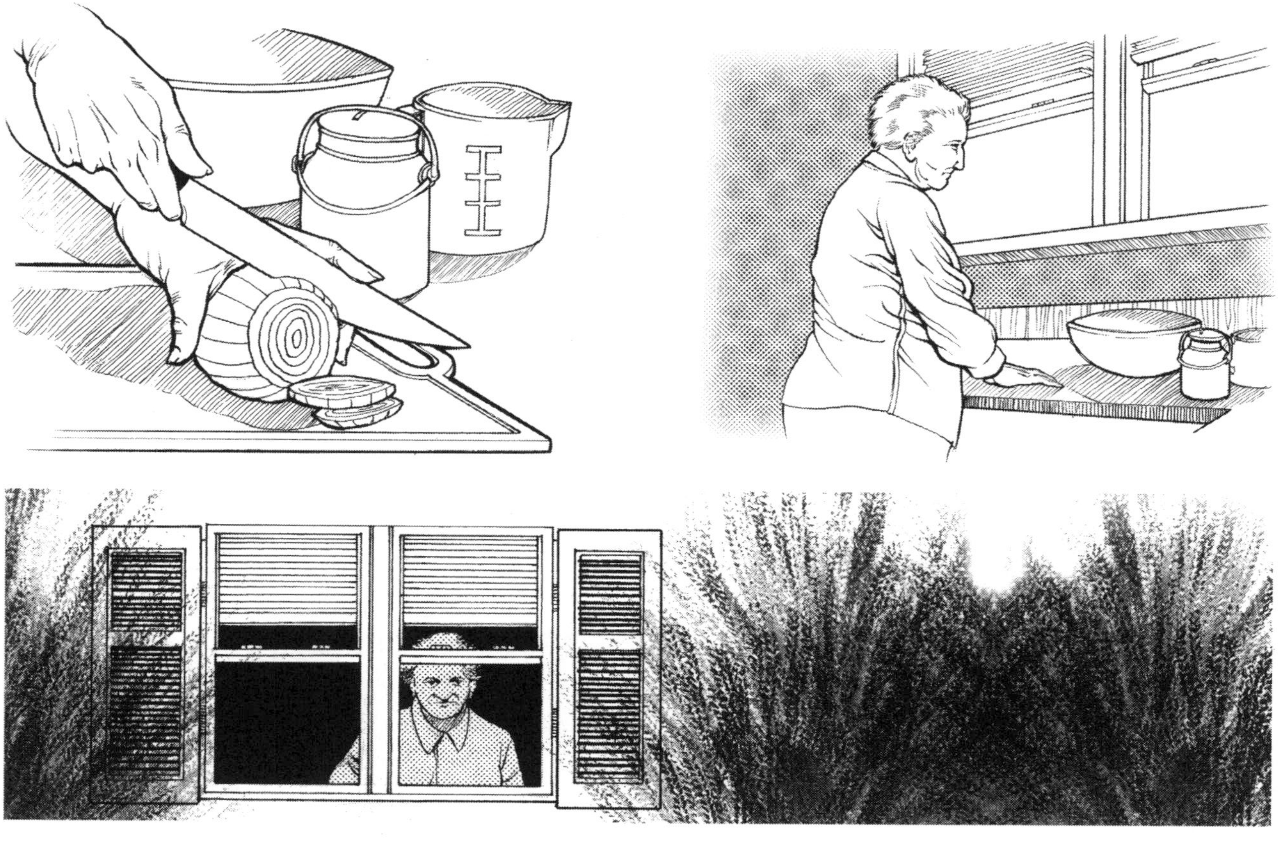

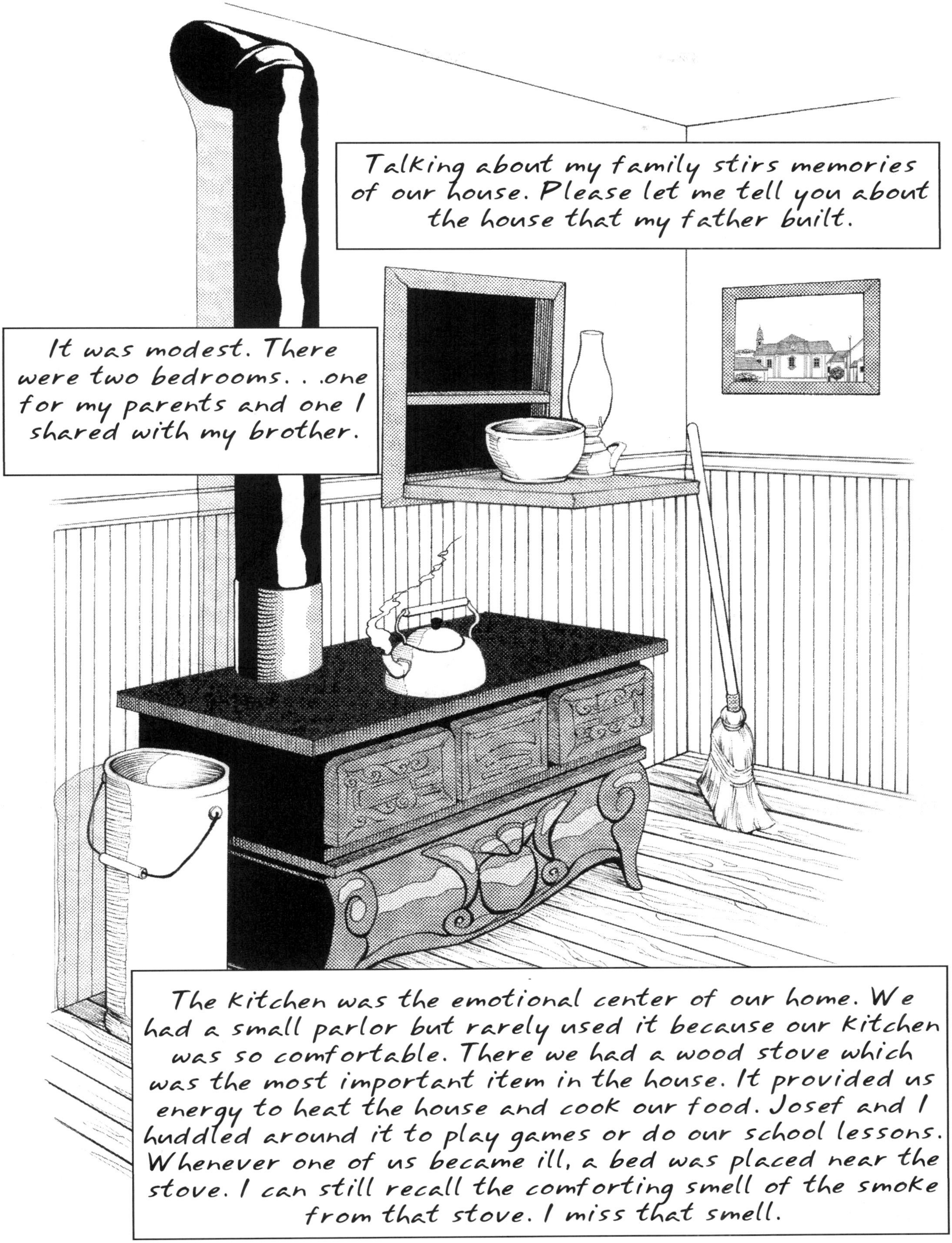
Talking about my family stirs memories of our house. Please let me tell you about the house that my father built.
It was modest. There were two bedrooms. . .one for my parents and one I shared with my brother.
The kitchen was the emotional center of our home. We had a small parlor but rarely used it because our kitchen was so comfortable. There we had a wood stove which was the most important item in the house. It provided us energy to heat the house and cook our food. Josef and I huddled around it to play games or do our school lessons. Whenever one of us became ill, a bed was placed near the stove. I can still recall the comforting smell of the smoke from that stove. I miss that smell.

My father built our house next to the Horak family farmstead. My uncle Stanislav lived on and ran the farm with his wife Anastazie. My aunt and uncle were childless, so as children Josef and I, along with our Horak cousins, would go there to ride horses and help with the farm work.

My memories of the farmstead are conflicted, understandably. I often experience memories of my time on the farmstead as if in still photographs. Maybe it is easier that way. It allows me to replace the real still photos of the horror that was to happen there later with my happier, gentler memories.

On our farmstead, as with most in Lidice, the women worked the fields. This was because many of the men worked in the mines and steelworks in Kladno.

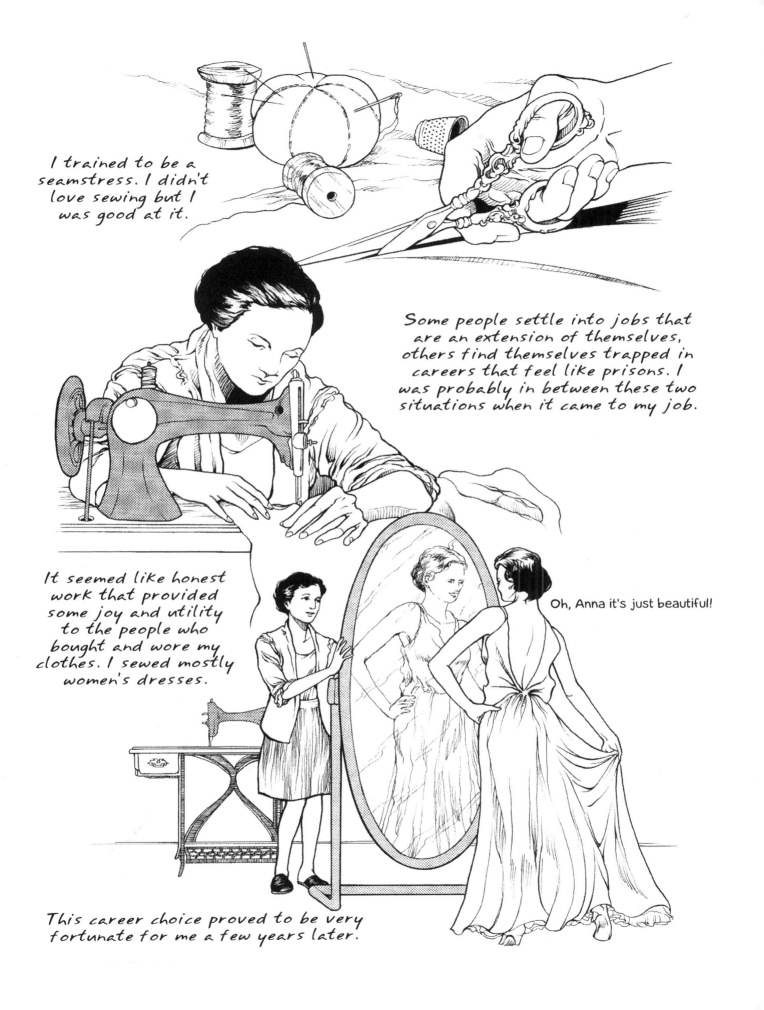

I trained to be a seamstress. I didn't love sewing but I was good at it.

Some people settle into jobs that are an extension of themselves, others find themselves trapped in careers that feel like prisons. I was probably in between these two situations when it came to my job.

It seemed like honest work that provided some joy and utility to the people who bought and wore my clothes. I sewed mostly women's dresses.

Oh, Anna it's just beautiful!

This career choice proved to be very fortunate for me a few years later.

There were a few professionals in Lidice, but most were tradespeople, laborers. I remember a handful of lawyers and government clerks, and one doctor, Dr. Jerabek.

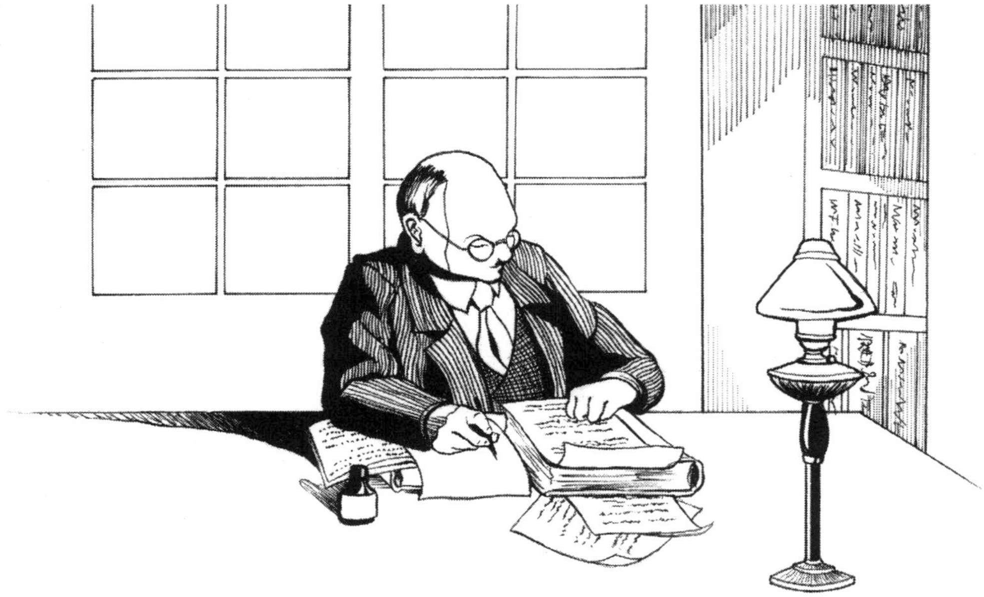

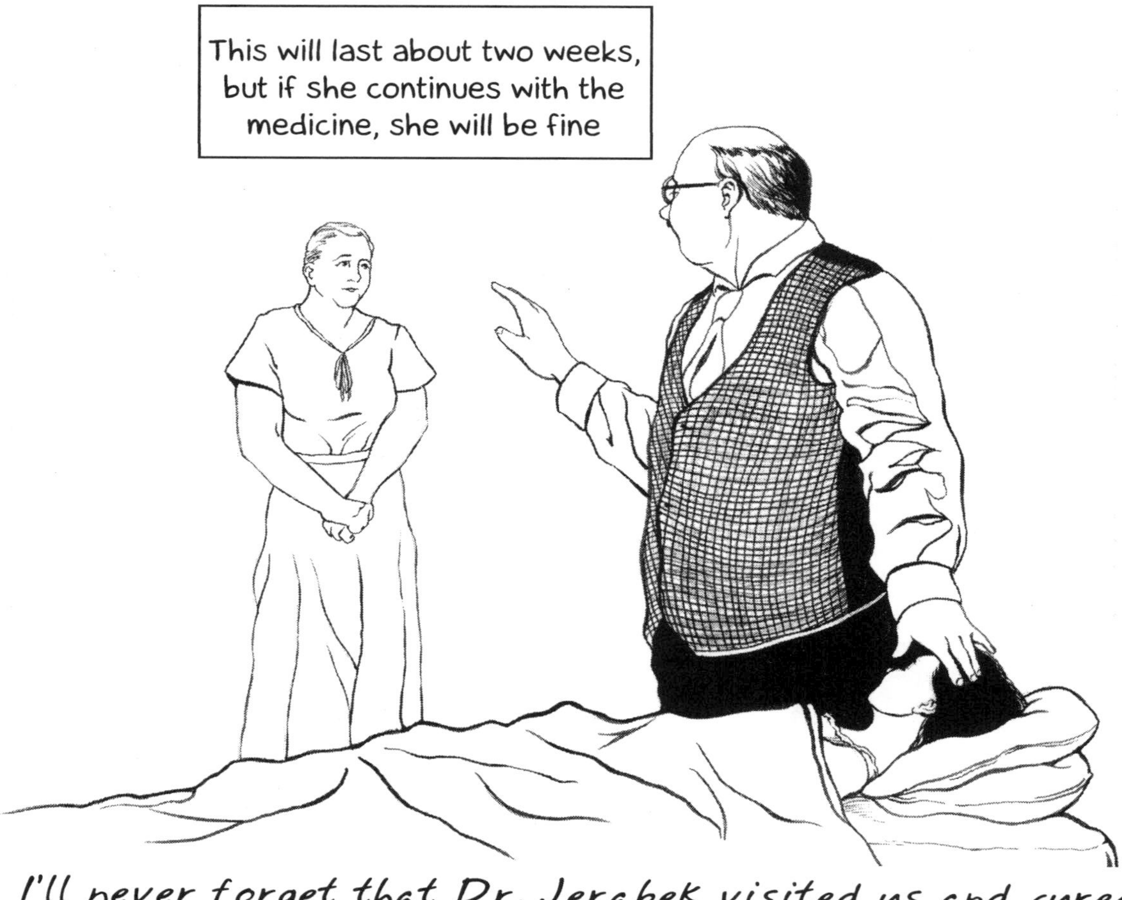
This will last about two weeks, but if she continues with the medicine, she will be fine

I'll never forget that Dr. Jerabek visited us and cured me when I had scarlet fever as a child. He also loved directing the church choir on Sundays and holidays.

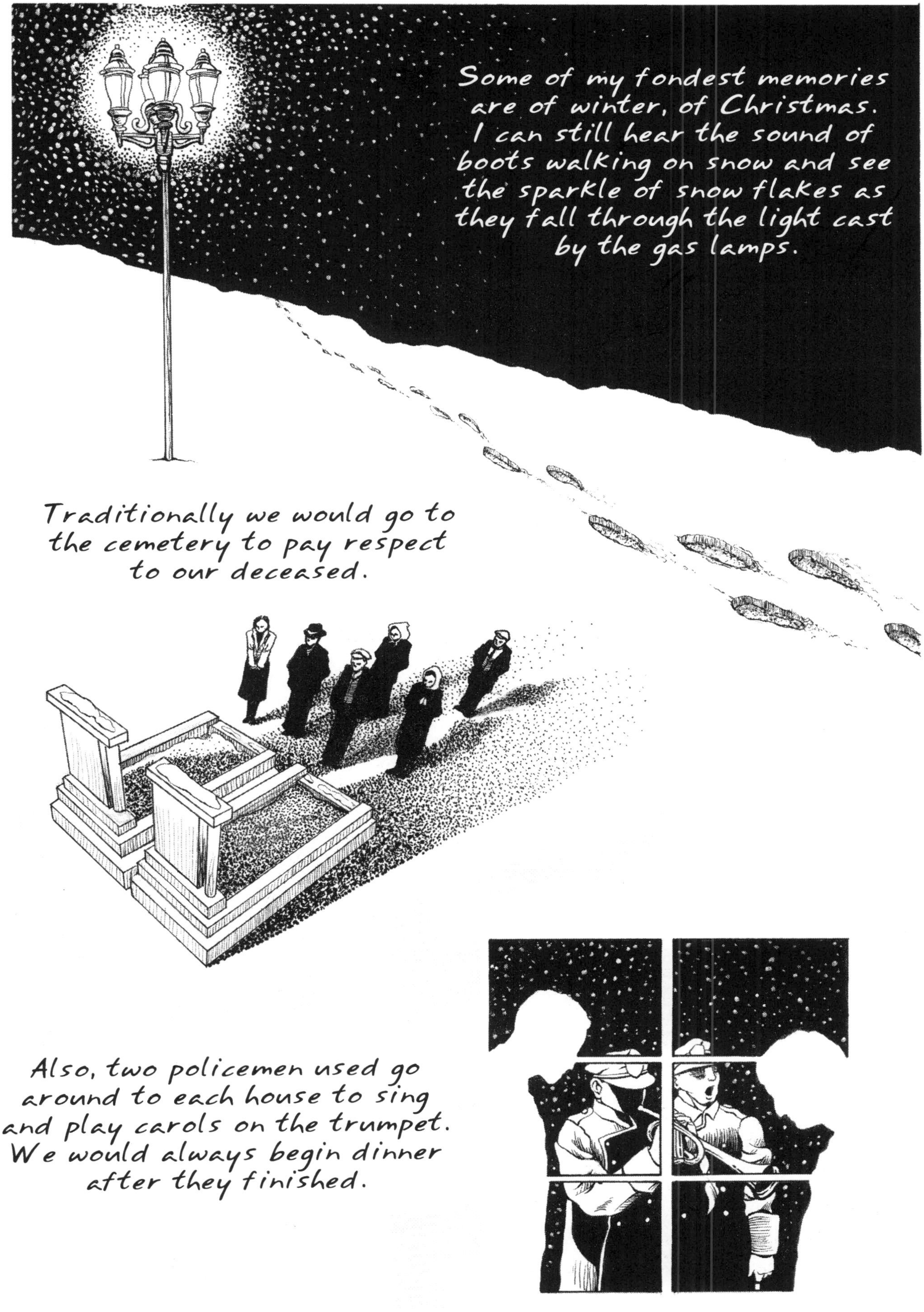
Some of my fondest memories are of winter, of Christmas. I can still hear the sound of boots walking on snow and see the sparkle of snow flakes as they fall through the light cast by the gas lamps.
Traditionally we would go to the cemetery to pay respect to our deceased.
Also, two policemen used go around to each house to sing and play carols on the trumpet. We would always begin dinner after they finished.

The main dish of a traditional Czech Christmas dinner is carp, usually bought live from fish mongers at an outdoor Christmas market.

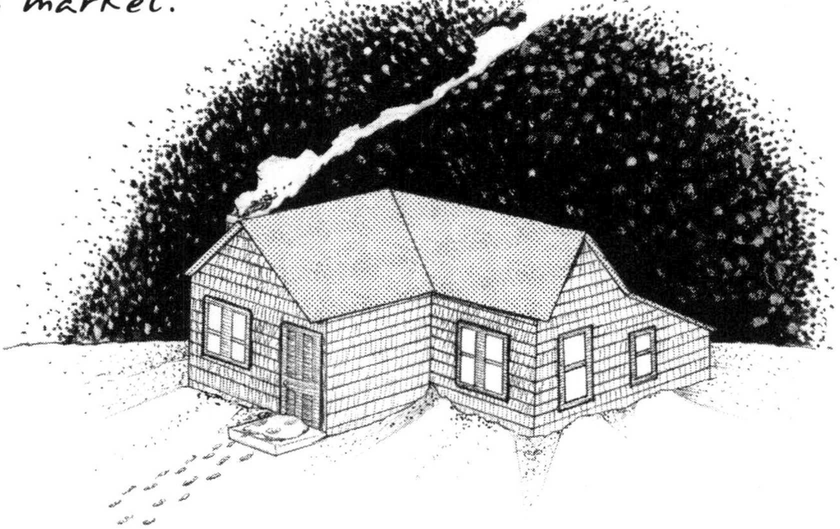

My family, however, rarely had carp at Christmas because my father hated it. We often had rabbit or chicken instead. Dinner concluded with a Christmas cake and then we exchanged gifts. A special Christmas smell was in the air all day.

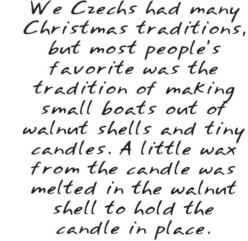

We Czechs had many Christmas traditions, but most people's favorite was the tradition of making small boats out of walnut shells and tiny candles. A little wax from the candle was melted in the walnut shell to hold the candle in place.

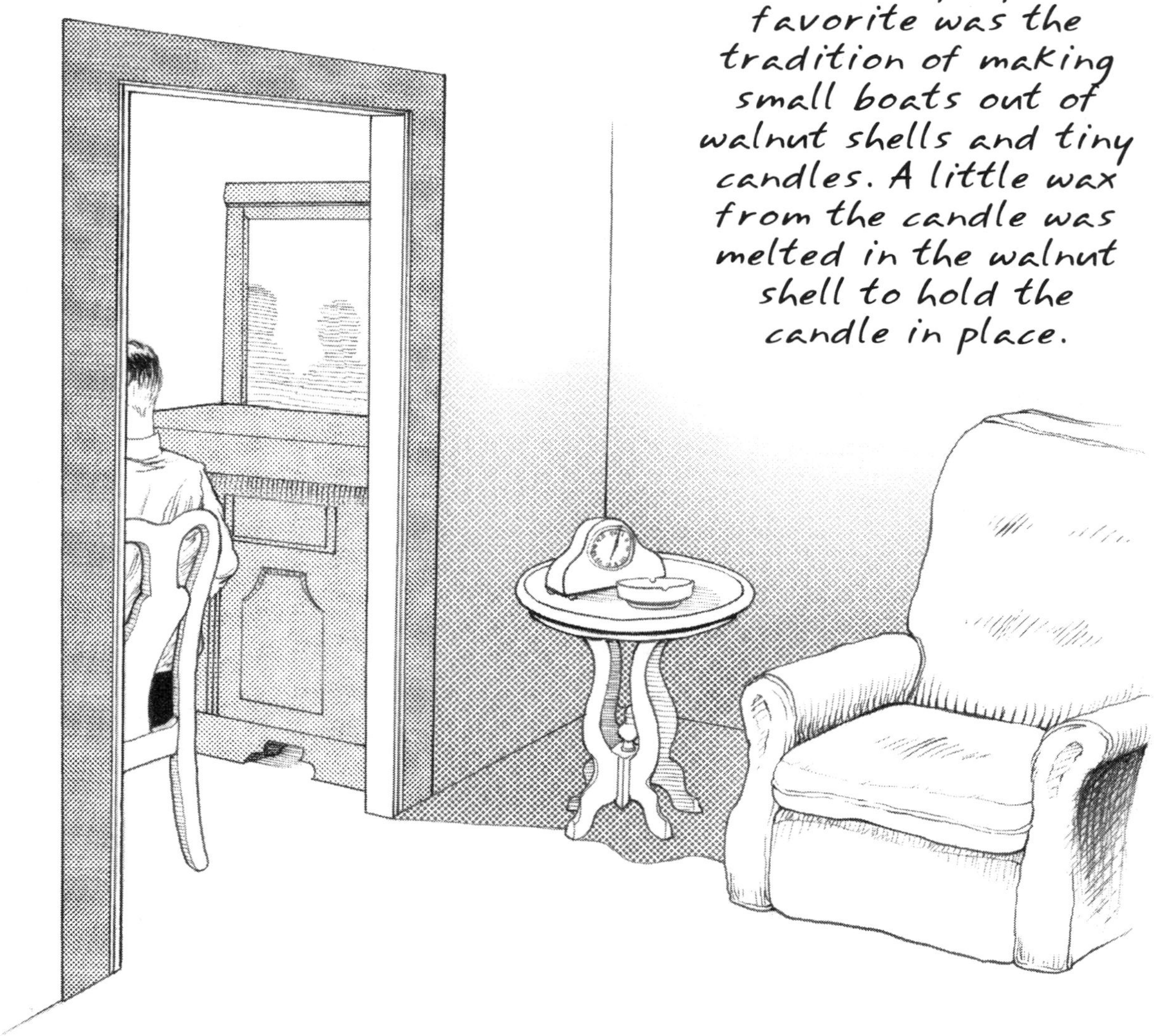

When every person had finished making a little walnut boat, each of the tiny candles was lighted, and the boats were placed in a large bowl of water. The way the boats floated foretold what was to happen in each person's life in the coming year.

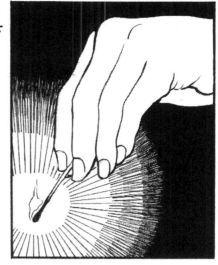

Boats which floated together signified that those people would be together in the year to come.

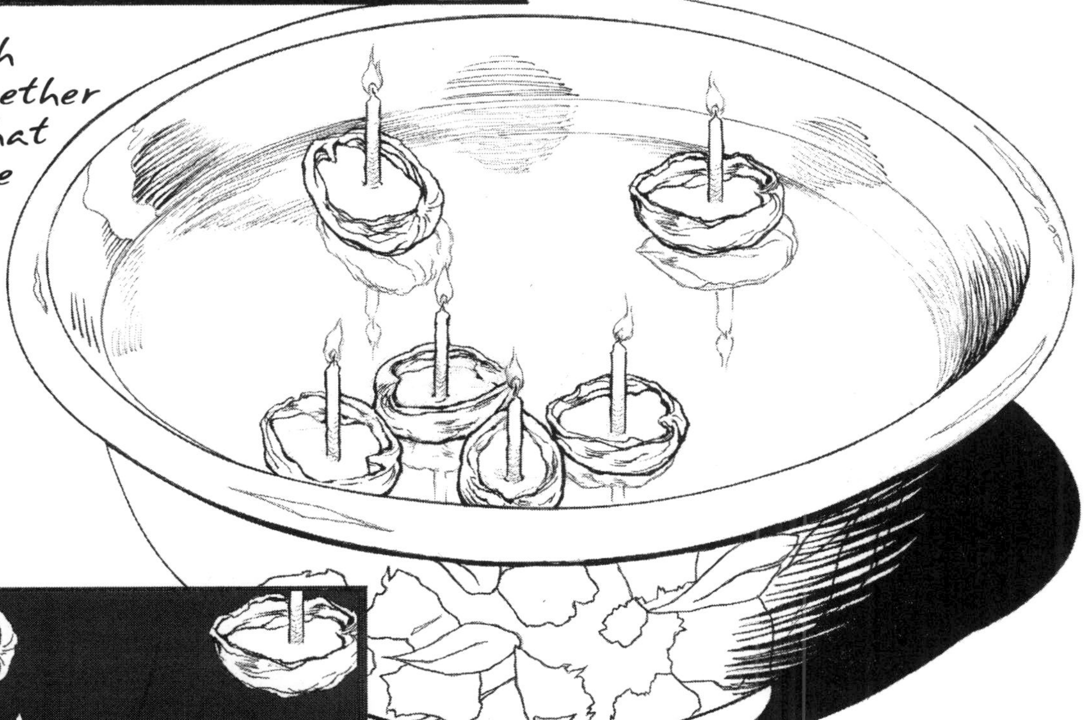

Boats which separated from the group would be apart from the rest that year.

If one's boat sank or one's candle went out, it meant tragedy was in the offing.

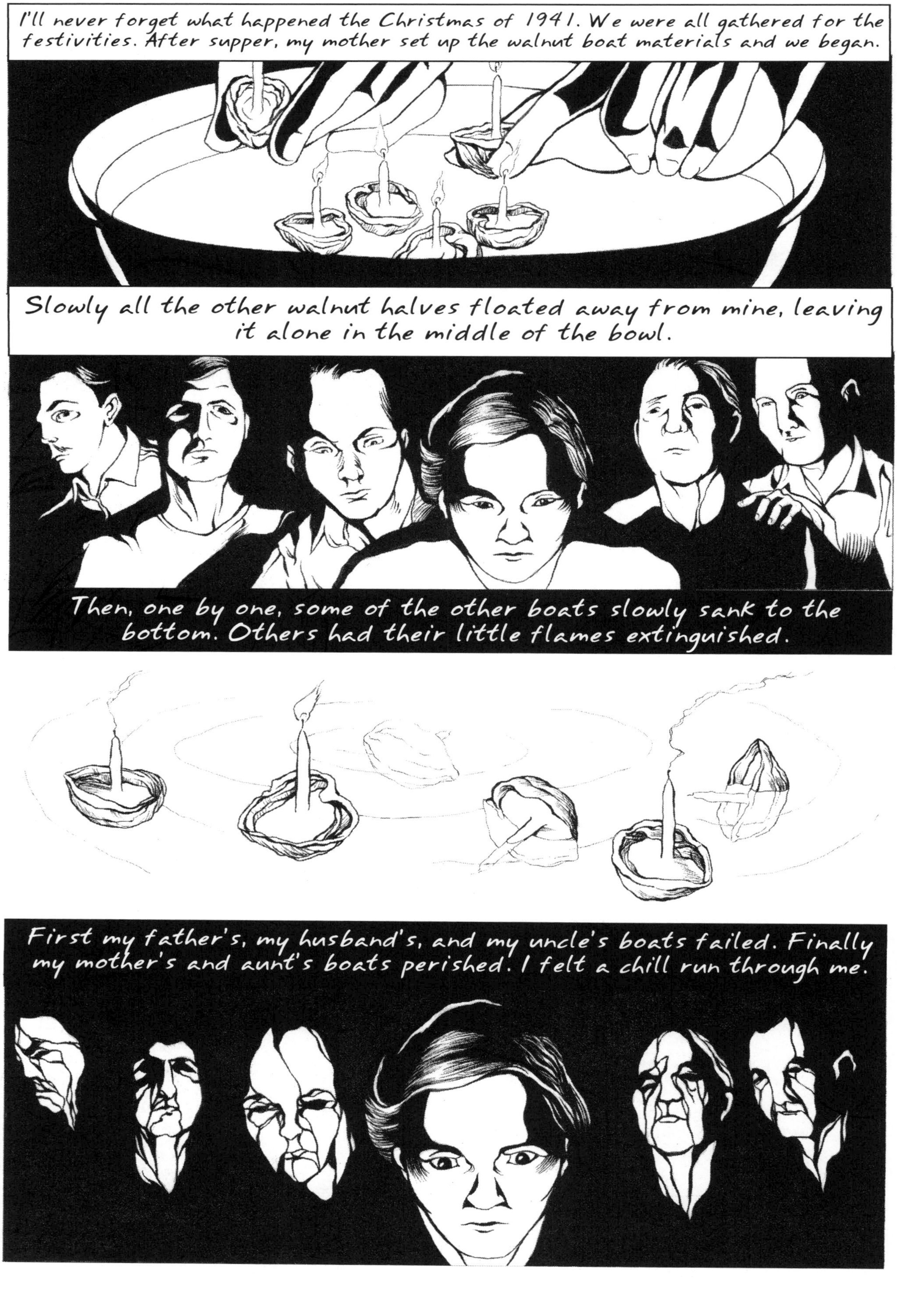
I'll never forget what happened the Christmas of 1941. We were all gathered for the festivities. After supper, my mother set up the walnut boat materials and we began.
Slowly all the other walnut halves floated away from mine, leaving it alone in the middle of the bowl.
Then, one by one, some of the other boats slowly sank to the bottom. Others had their little flames extinguished.
First my father's, my husband's, and my uncle's boats failed. Finally my mother's and aunt's boats perished. I felt a chill run through me.

There was nervous laughter around the room, and uncle Stanislav made some morbid joke to lighten the mood. We all moved on to other Christmas eve activities, but the unease hung in the air until the end of the evening. The feelings of this moment have stayed fresh in my body for all the years ever since.

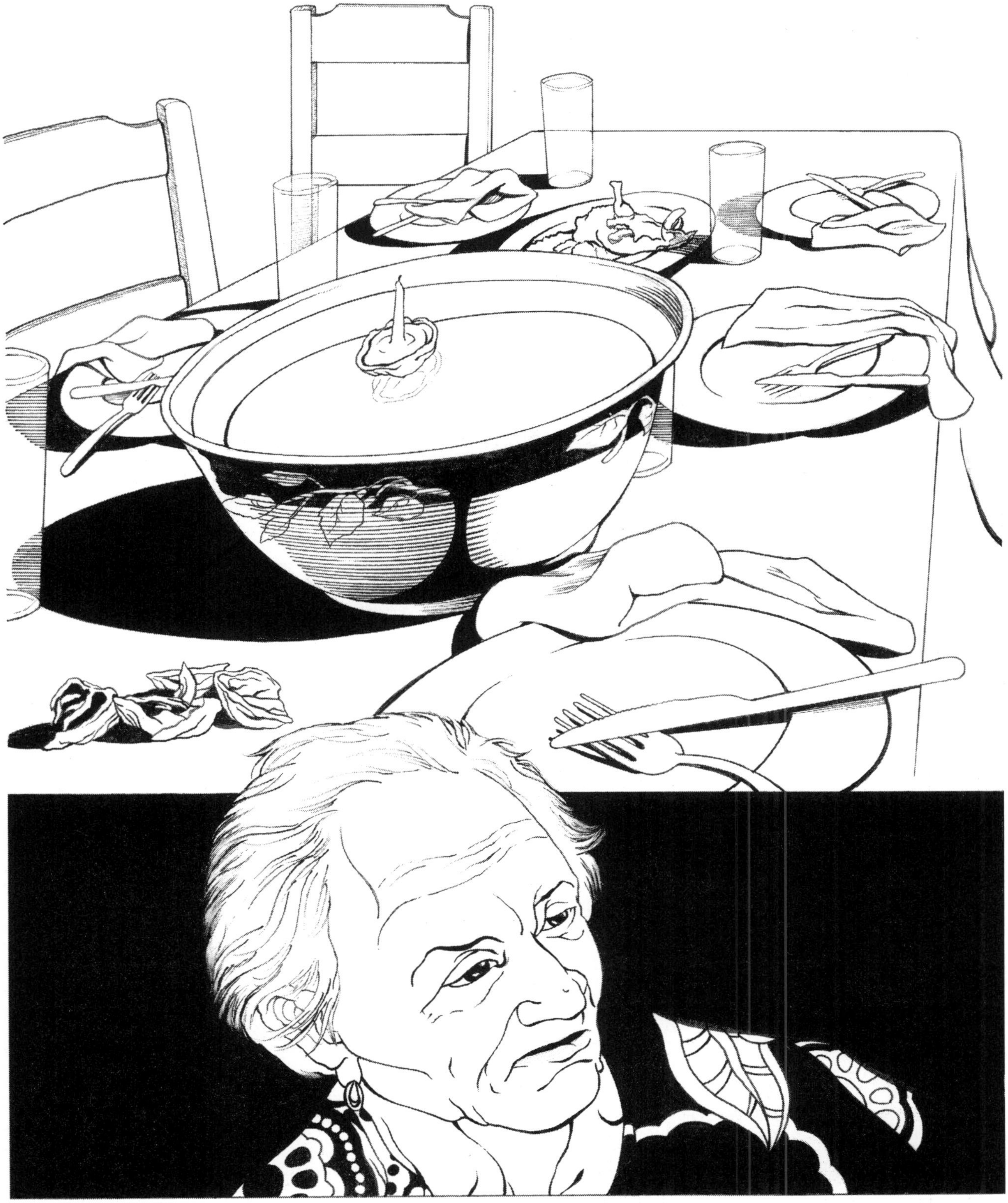

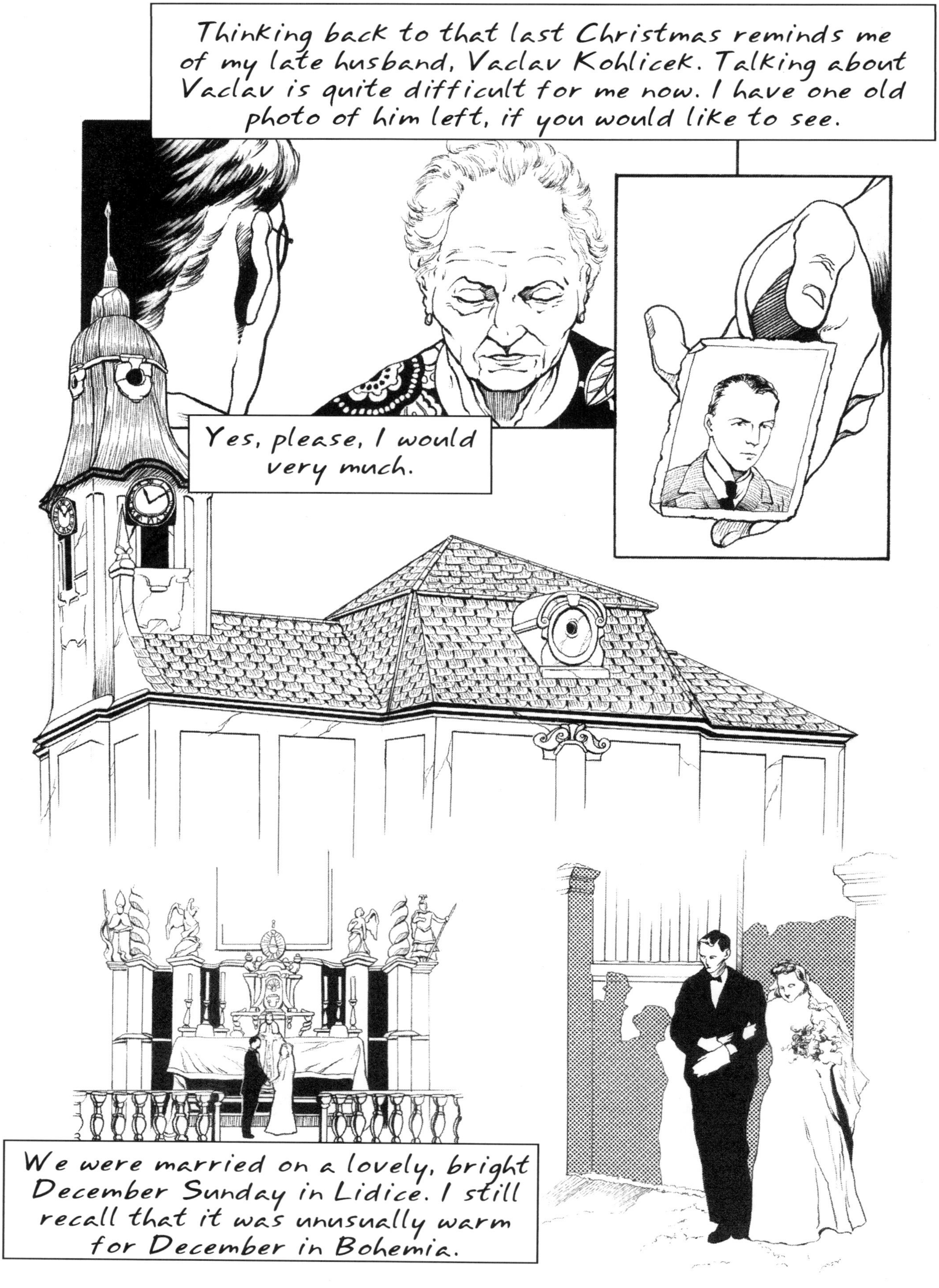
Thinking back to that last Christmas reminds me of my late husband, Vaclav Kohlicek. Talking about Vaclav is quite difficult for me now. I have one old photo of him left, if you would like to see.
Yes, please, I would very much.
We were married on a lovely, bright December Sunday in Lidice. I still recall that it was unusually warm for December in Bohemia.

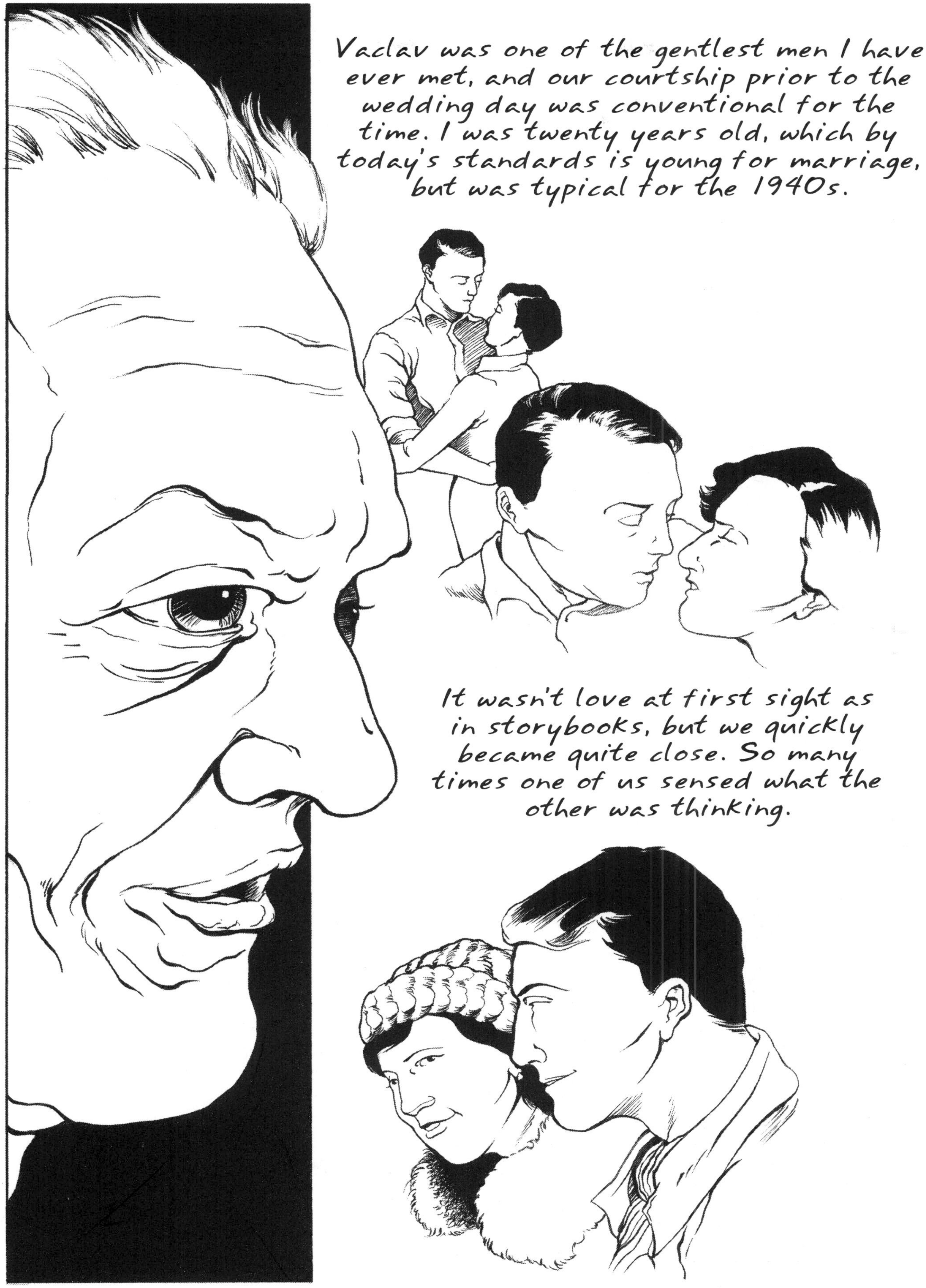
Vaclav was one of the gentlest men I have ever met, and our courtship prior to the wedding day was conventional for the time. I was twenty years old, which by today's standards is young for marriage, but was typical for the 1940s.
It wasn't love at first sight as in storybooks, but we quickly became quite close. So many times one of us sensed what the other was thinking.

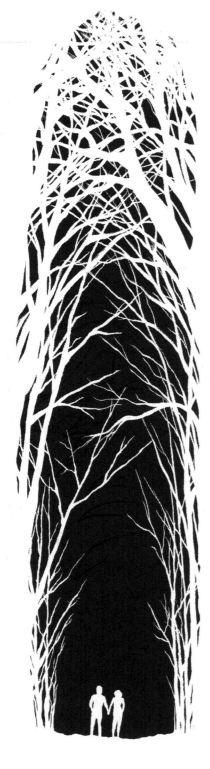

We often took long walks in the woods outside our village. Vaclav loved to explain the nature we came across on our strolls. His passion for such things was infectious.

He particularly loved going mushroom picking in the forests near Lidice. This is a kind of national pastime for Czechs and Vaclav was no different. I was less interested in mushrooming than him, but I always looked forward to our walks.

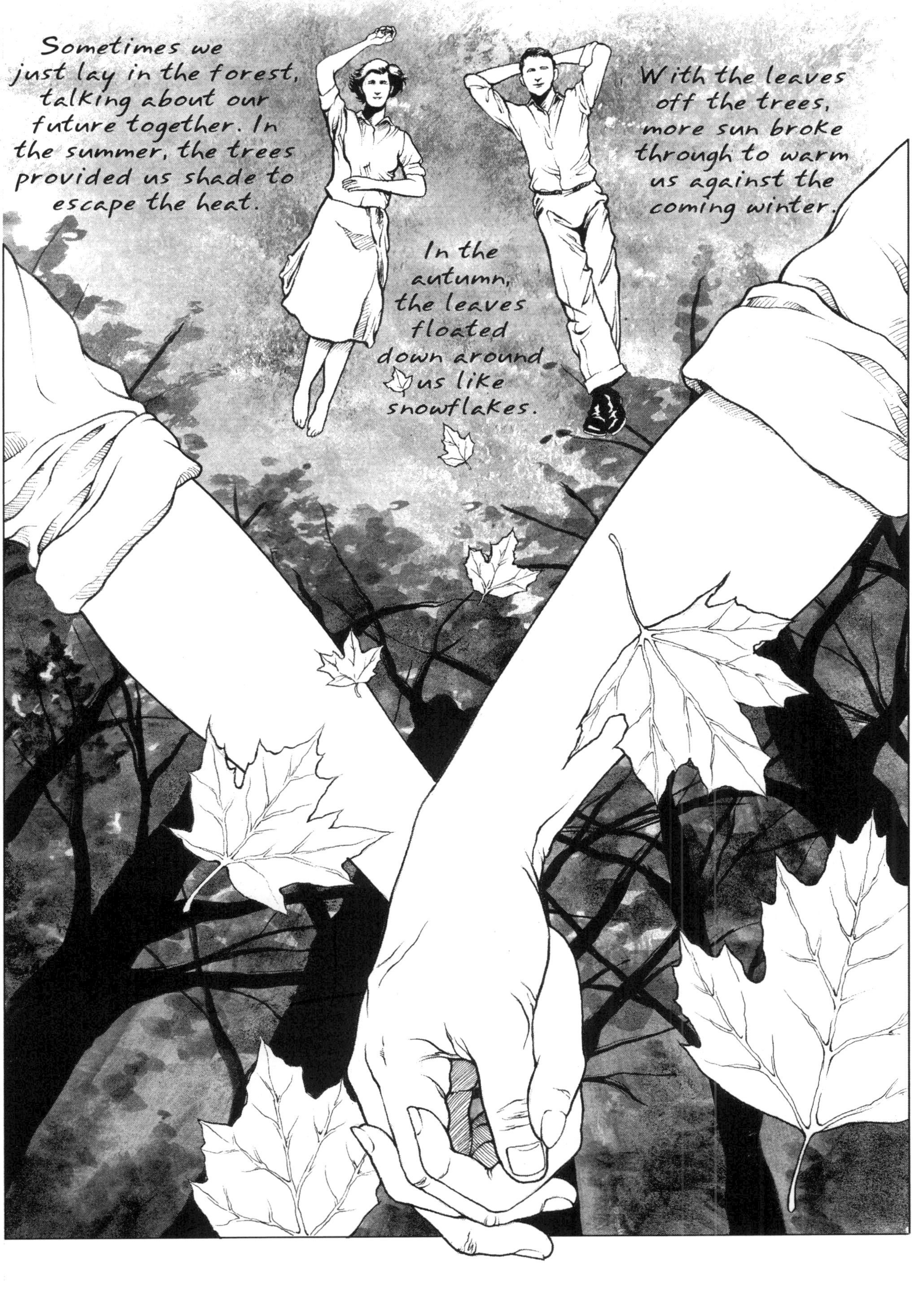
Sometimes we just lay in the forest, talking about our future together. In the summer, the trees provided us shade to escape the heat.
In the autumn, the leaves floated down around us like snowflakes.
With the leaves off the trees, more sun broke through to warm us against the coming winter.

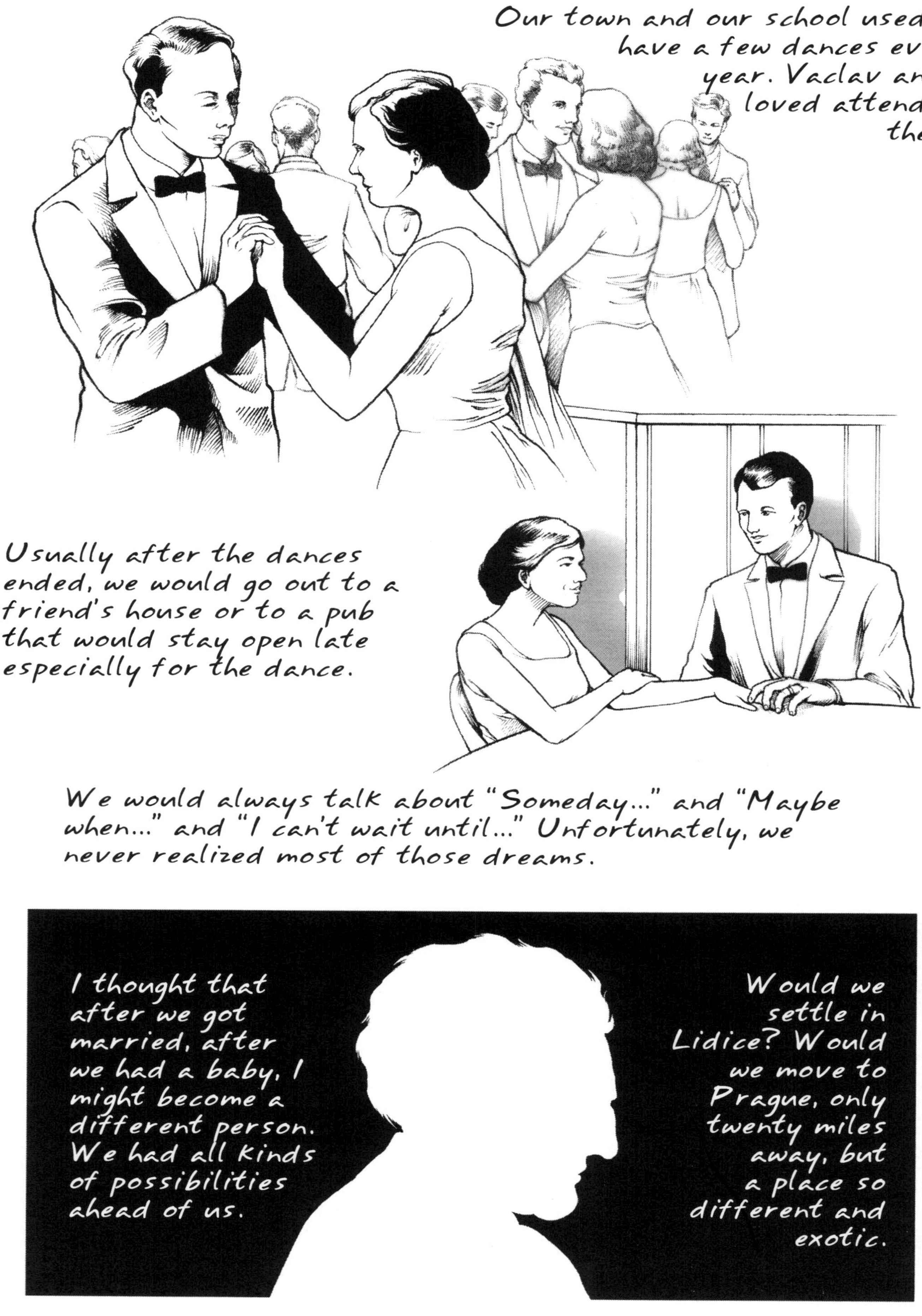
Our town and our school used to have a few dances every year. Vaclav and I loved attending these.
Usually after the dances ended, we would go out to a friend's house or to a pub that would stay open late especially for the dance.
We would always talk about "Someday..." and "Maybe when..." and "I can't wait until..." Unfortunately, we never realized most of those dreams.
I thought that after we got married, after we had a baby, I might become a different person. We had all kinds of possibilities ahead of us.
Would we settle in Lidice? Would we move to Prague, only twenty miles away, but a place so different and exotic.

Soon after we were married, we decided to start a family. Perhaps we were too young to make such an important decision, but both of our families supported us.

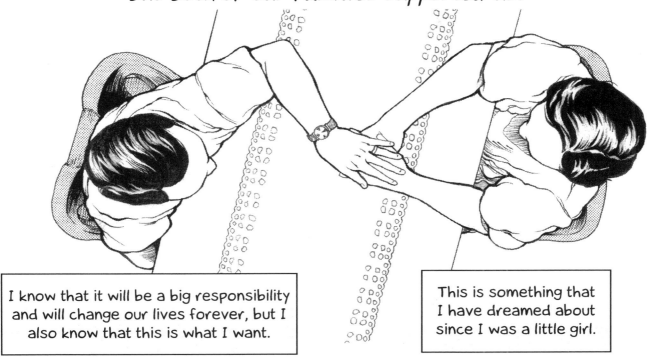

I know that it will be a big responsibility and will change our lives forever, but I also know that this is what I want.

This is something that I have dreamed about since I was a little girl.

I am pleased to give you the good news. You're pregnant!

Doctor, thank you so much!

We struggled at first, but were eventually successful when I became pregnant in the autumn of 1941. I had no idea how important and ultimately tragic my pregnancy would become.

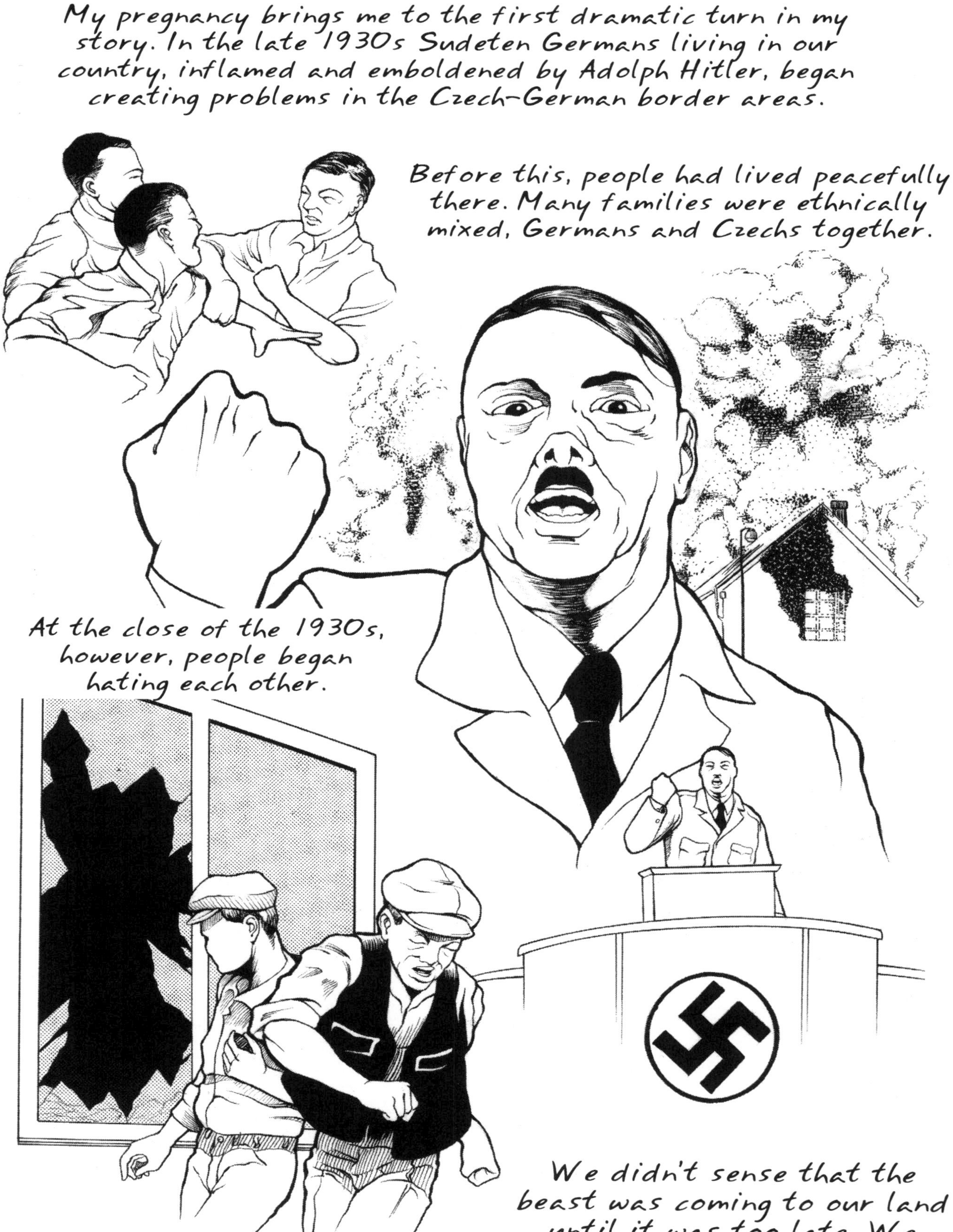
My pregnancy brings me to the first dramatic turn in my story. In the late 1930s Sudeten Germans living in our country, inflamed and emboldened by Adolph Hitler, began creating problems in the Czech-German border areas.
Before this, people had lived peacefully there. Many families were ethnically mixed, Germans and Czechs together.
At the close of the 1930s, however, people began hating each other.
We didn't sense that the beast was coming to our land until it was too late. We counted on the protection of others. We were naive.

Then the Munich Conference happened in June of 1938 and a decision was made about us without us. When Neville Chamberlain and Edouard Daladier signed us away to Hitler, what were we to do? Chamberlain and Daladier cared about Britain and France, maybe even western Europe, but they sacrificed our small nation, and now everyone sees the results.

Our president, Edvard Benes, decided not to fight, which was wise. How could we resist such numerical superiority? Besides, nobody anticipated what was coming.

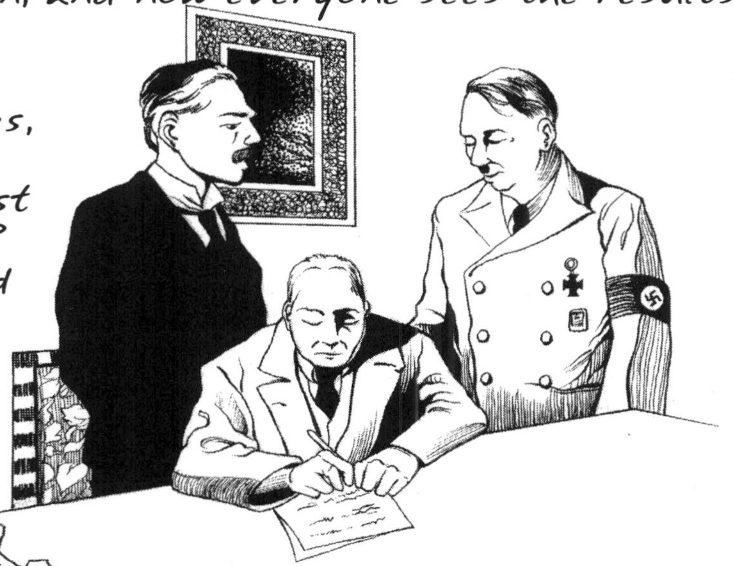

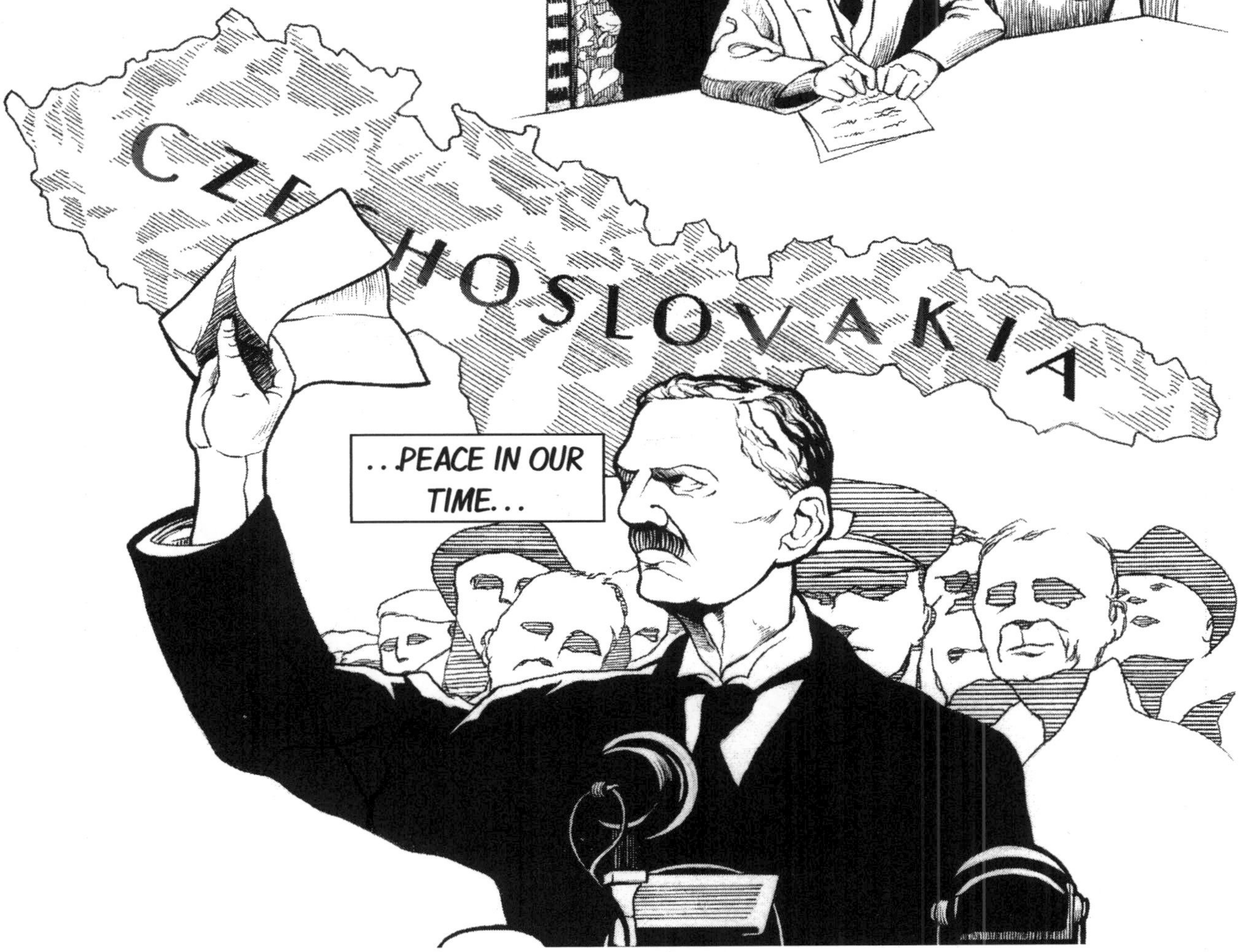
CZE
HOSLOVAKIA
...PEACE IN OUR TIME...

Once we realized what was in the offing, even in our daily routines, there was a persistent sense that something tragic was about to transpire, like the feeling one gets when seeing a careless child run into the street. We were anticipating the crunching blow that we were sure would come, even as we hoped it wouldn't.

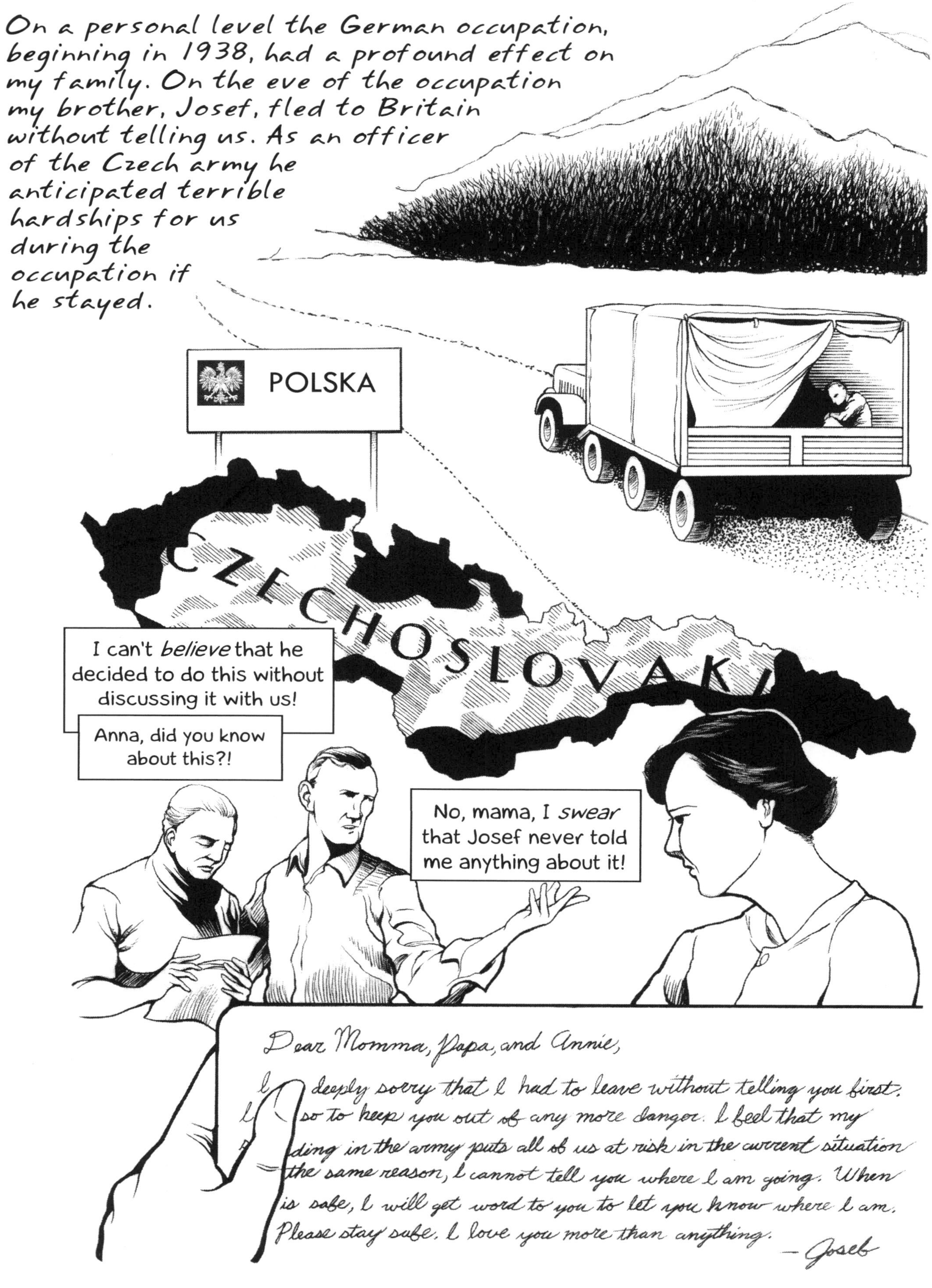
On a personal level the German occupation, beginning in 1938, had a profound effect on my family. On the eve of the occupation my brother, Josef, fled to Britain without telling us. As an officer of the Czech army he anticipated terrible hardships for us during the occupation if he stayed.
POLSKA
CZECHOSLOVAKI
I can't *believe* that he decided to do this without discussing it with us!
Anna, did you know about this?!
No, mama, I *swear* that Josef never told me anything about it!
Dear Momma, Papa, and Annie,
deeply sorry that I had to leave without telling you first.
so to keep you out of any more danger. I feel that my
ding in the army puts all of us at risk in the current situation
the same reason, I cannot tell you where I am going. When
is safe, I will get word to you to let you know where I am.
Please stay safe. I love you more than anything.
— Josef

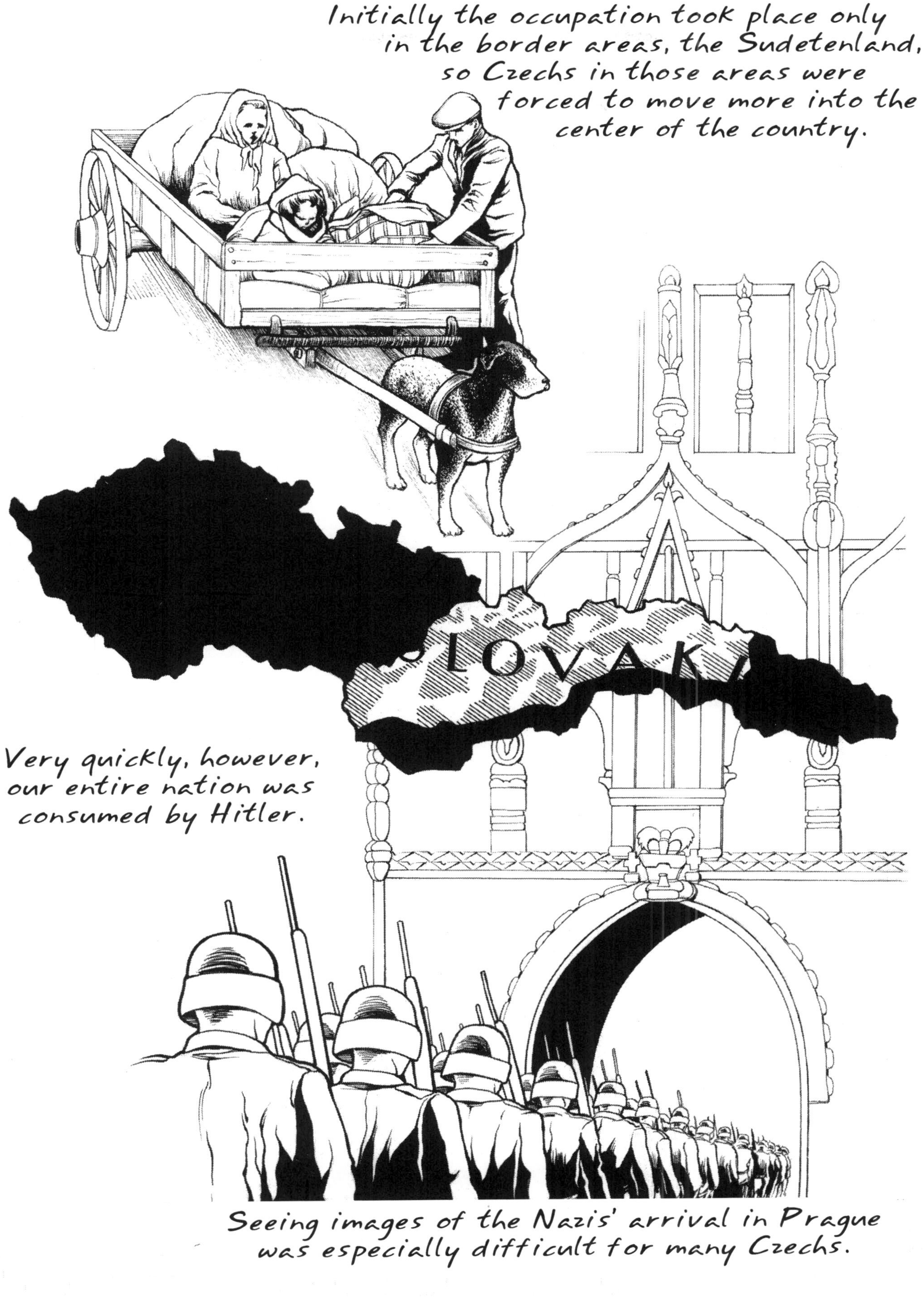
Initially the occupation took place only in the border areas, the Sudetenland, so Czechs in those areas were forced to move more into the center of the country.
Very quickly, however, our entire nation was consumed by Hitler.
Seeing images of the Nazis' arrival in Prague was especially difficult for many Czechs.

German soldiers moved into all regions. Homeowners were forced to provide shelter and board to the occupiers. Many of these "soldiers" were undernourished boys who were put with Czech families to gain weight and strength. They even took our food and sent it back to Germany.

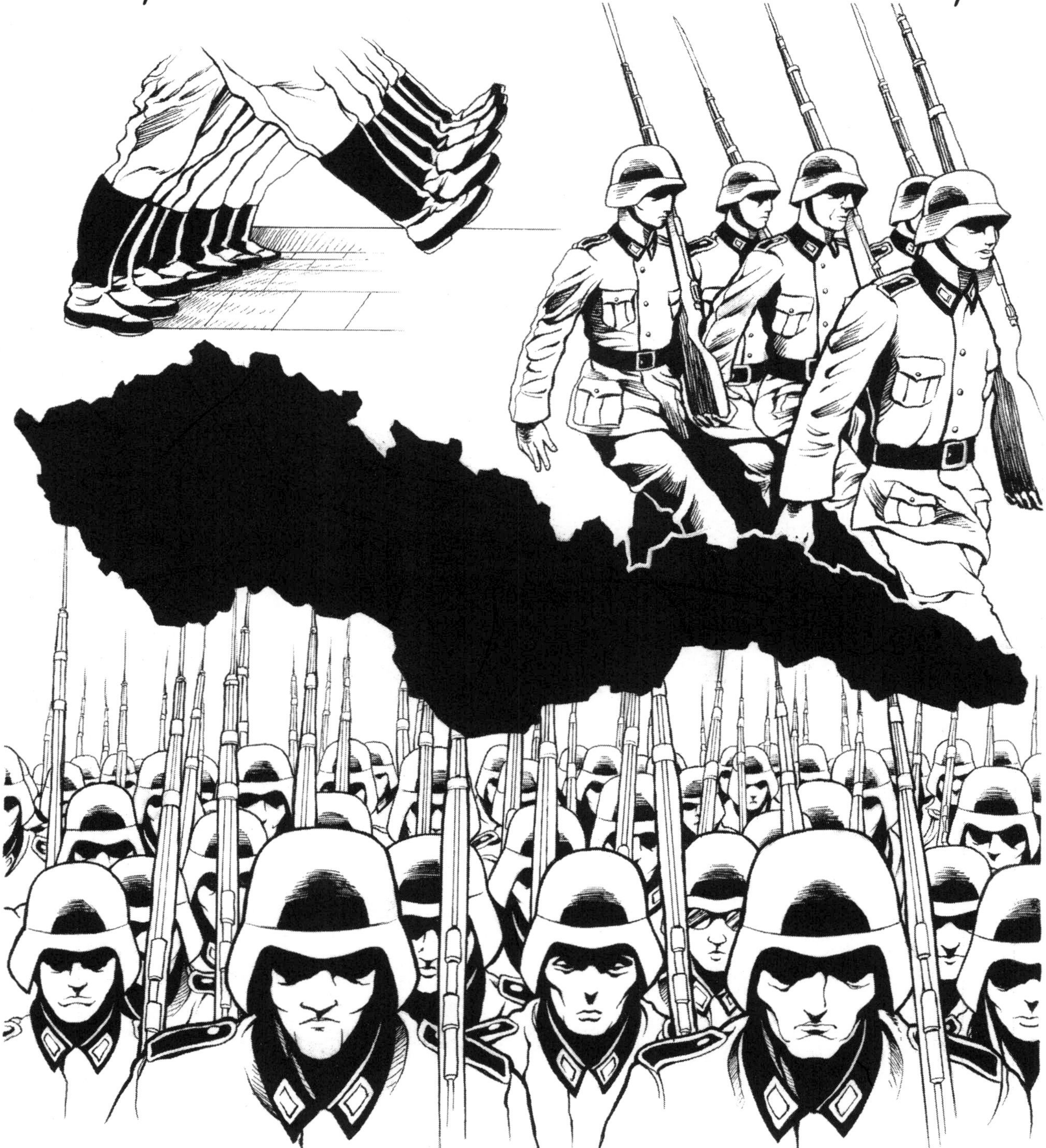

We all thought that this misery could not get worse. Then we were introduced to Heydrich.

Heydrich the hangman. The butcher of Prague. The blond beast. He was known by many names. Word of his coming spread from person-to-person, house-to-house, street-to-street.

While the man that Heydrich replaced, Konstantin von Neurath, and his SS assistant Karl Frank, were seen as cold bureaucrats who could be ruthless on occasion, Heydrich's brutal reputation was legendary.

The first newspaper photo of Heydrich that I saw was chilling. The deceptively kind eyes of an executioner, the soft friendly lines of his face. I knew behind this lay a cold, black soul.

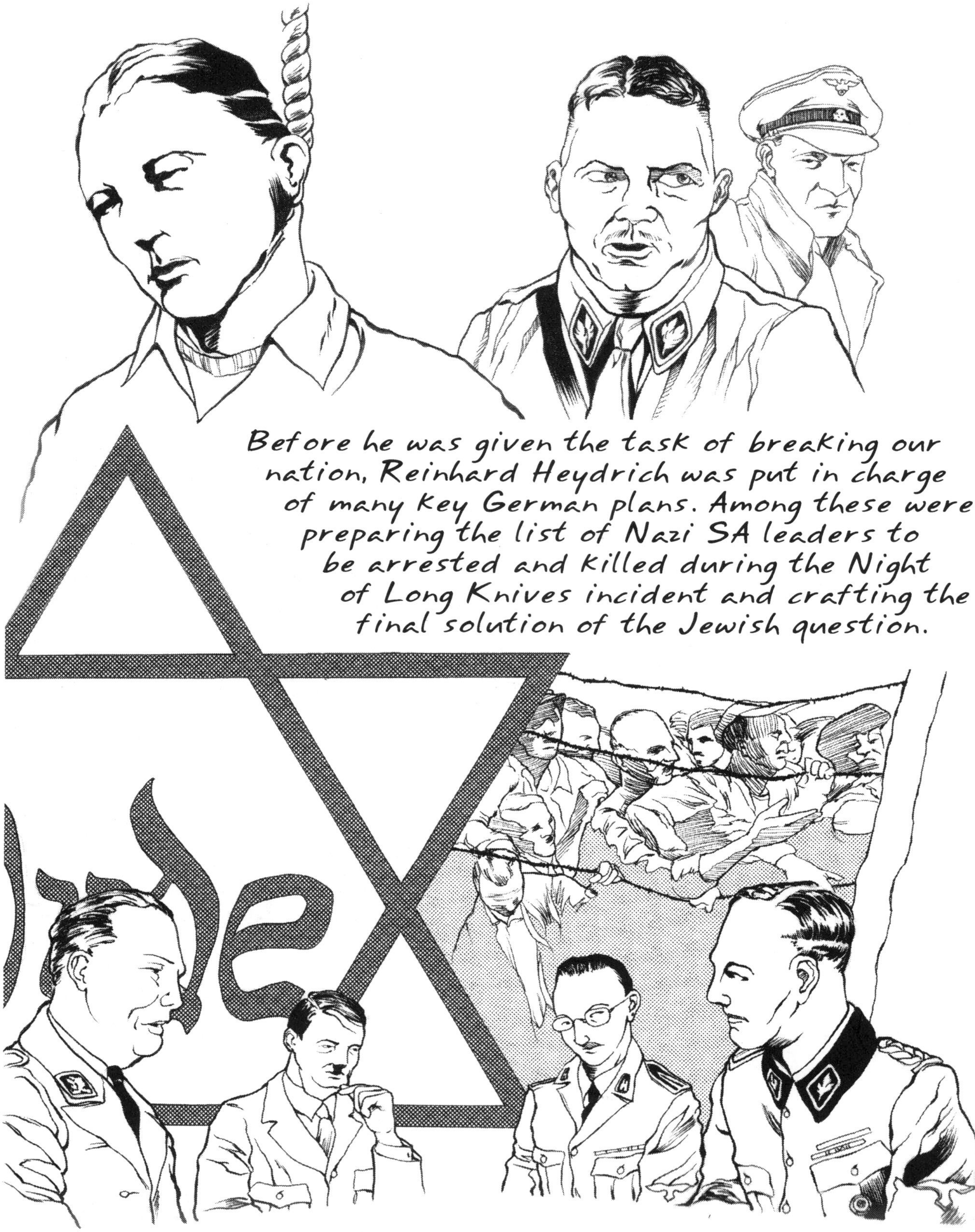
Before he was given the task of breaking our nation, Reinhard Heydrich was put in charge of many key German plans. Among these were preparing the list of Nazi SA leaders to be arrested and killed during the Night of Long Knives incident and crafting the final solution of the Jewish question.

This work had to be interrupted, however, when Hitler asked him to replace von Neurath, who the Nazi leadership felt was weak and inefficient in his administration of the occupation.

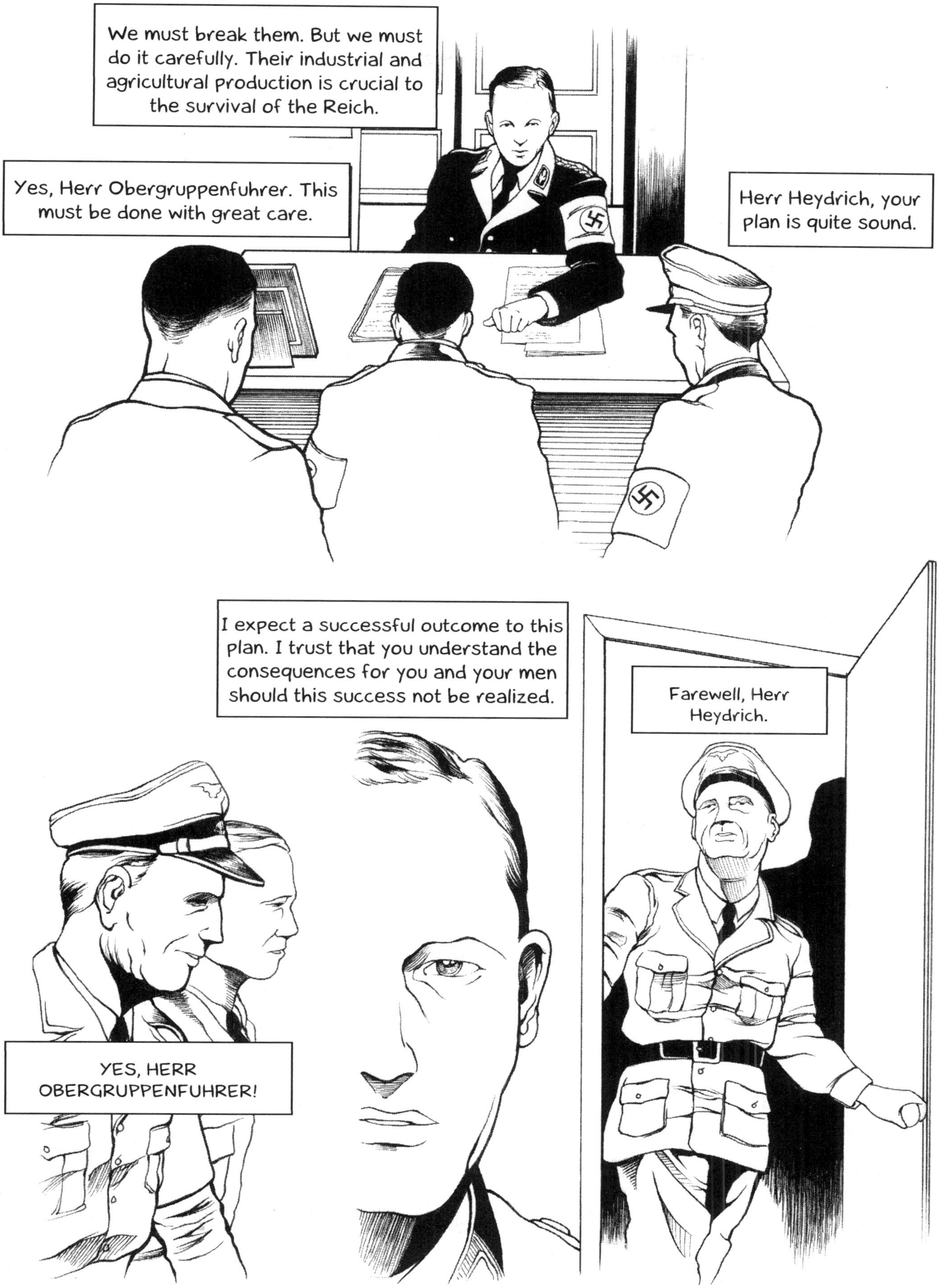
We must break them. But we must do it carefully. Their industrial and agricultural production is crucial to the survival of the Reich.
Yes, Herr Obergruppenfuhrer. This must be done with great care.
Herr Heydrich, your plan is quite sound.
I expect a successful outcome to this plan. I trust that you understand the consequences for you and your men should this success not be realized.
Farewell, Herr Heydrich.
YES, HERR OBERGRUPPENFUHRER!

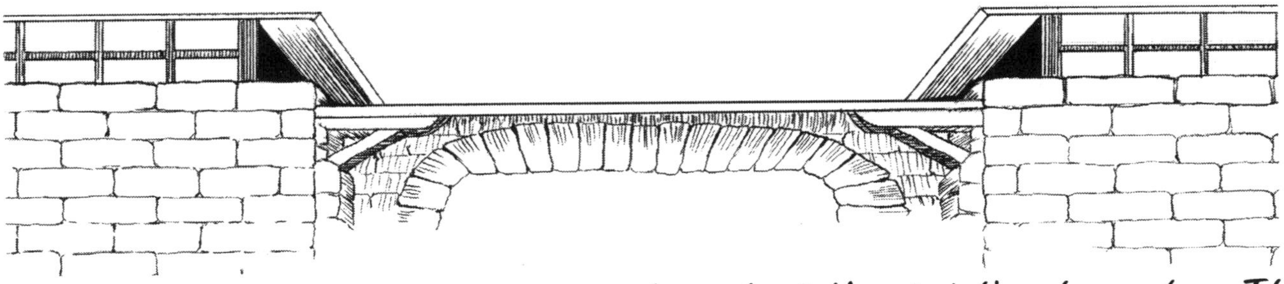

Inefficiency and weakness were not part of Heydrich's character. The first Czechs to suffer greatly during his reign were, of course, our Jewish population. Many of them were taken to the Terezin concentration camp in north Bohemia. I have read that out of a population of over 100,000 Jews in Czechoslovakia, fewer than 500 survived in hiding during the occupation. We mostly heard about this in Lidice because we didn't have any Jews in our village. At that point it was less real for us.

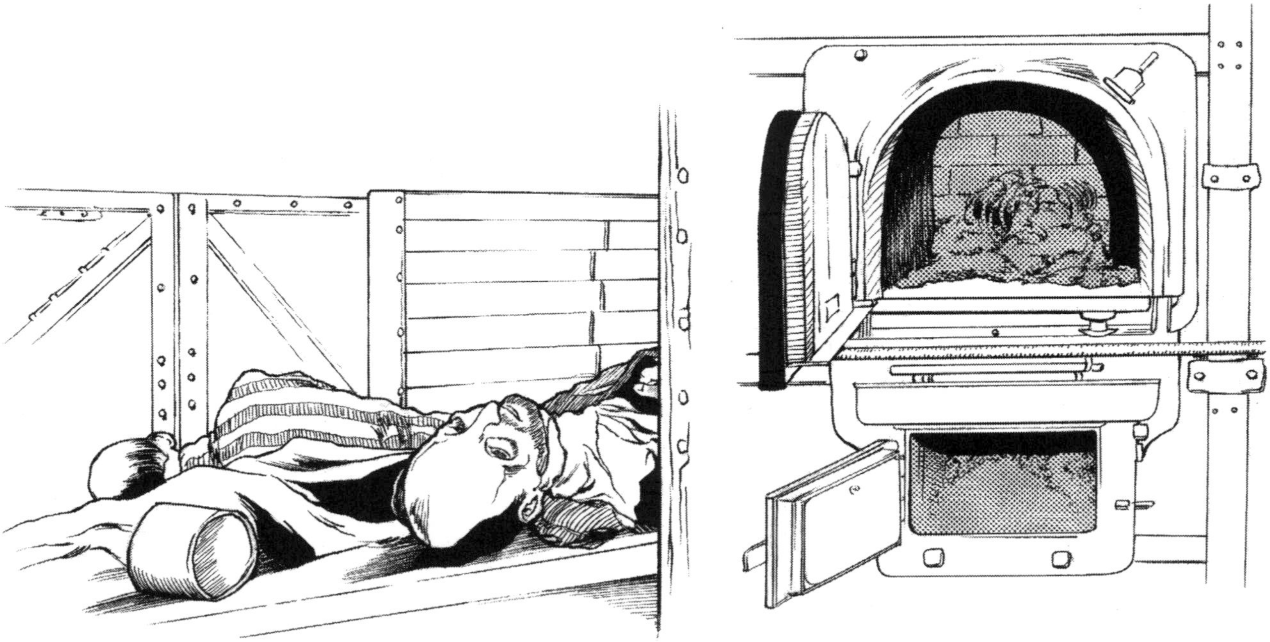

The terror was not limited to the Jews for long. Soon the general Czech population felt Heydrich's wrath. Thousands of Czechs were immediately sent to camps or summarily executed. Fear gripped the nation.

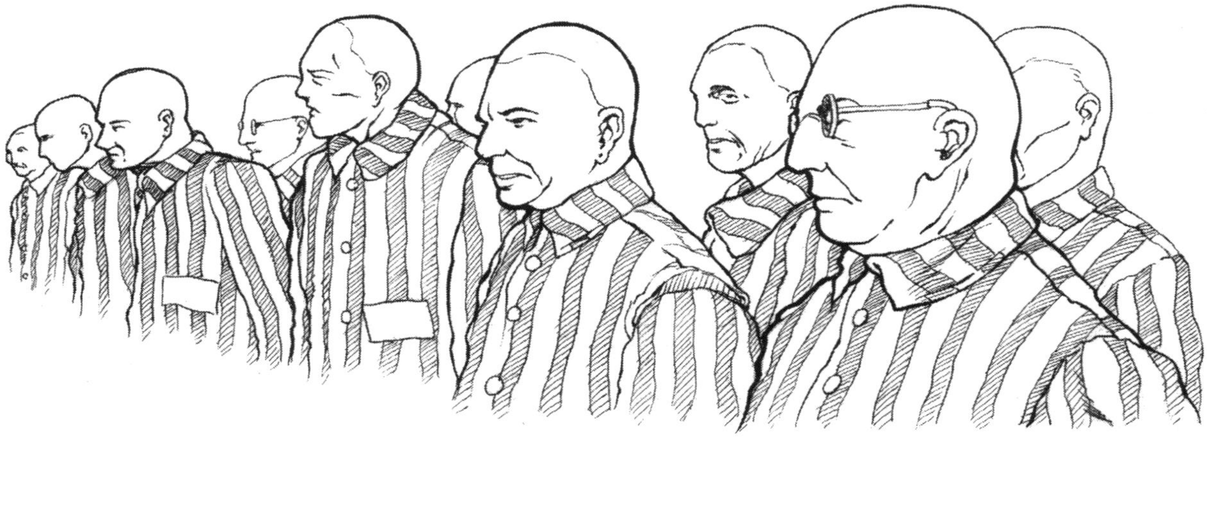

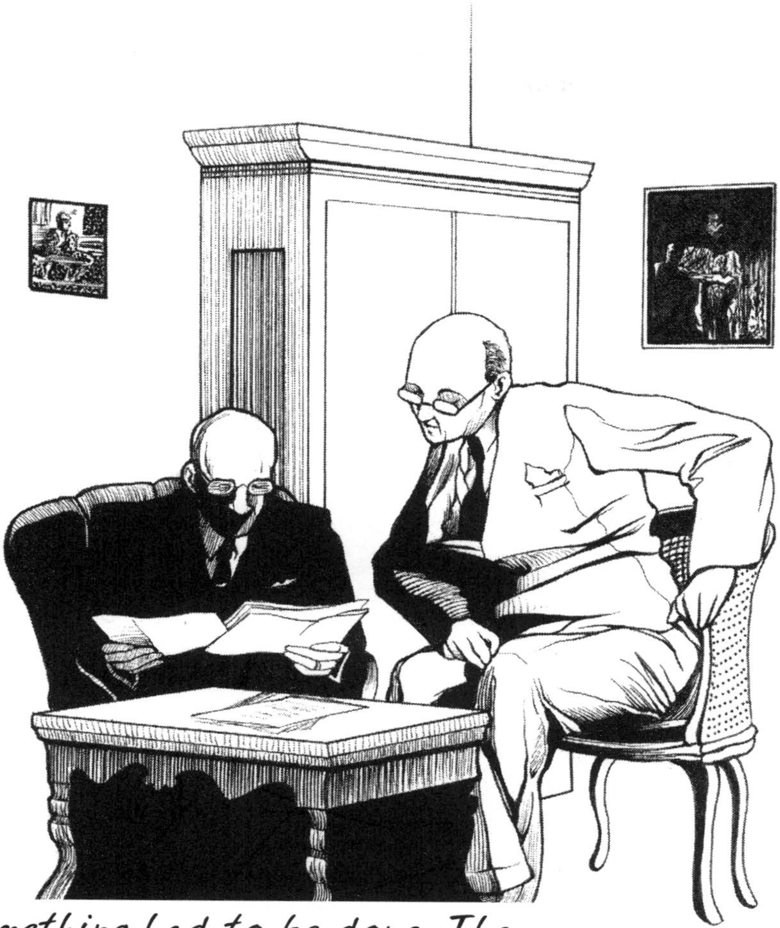

This escalation alarmed our government in exile, operating in London. Our president, Edvard Benes, and foreign secretary, Jan Masaryk, decided a more active resistance was necessary.

In hindsight we Czechs are very divided on whether his decision was wise. I still support it, even with the consequences it brought for my village and my family.

Something had to be done. The Germans were saying that Prague's Wenceslas Square would be paved with Czech heads. They were cutting a path of blood and bone through the soil of our nation.

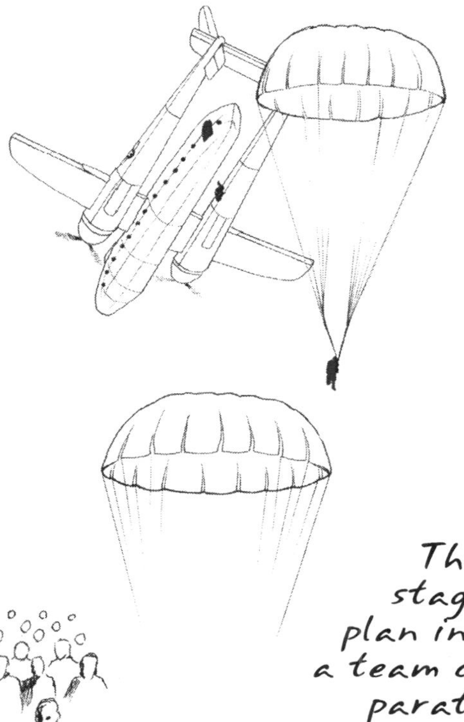

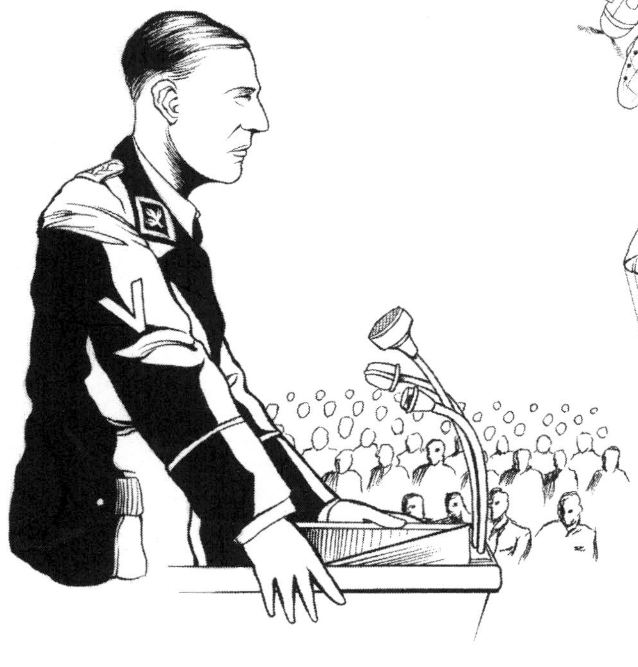

The initial stage of the plan invovlved a team of Czech paratroopers serving in the RAF in Britain.

I want to take a moment to talk on a personal level about Jan Masaryk and Edvard Benes. During my brother's time in England during the war, he and his family became very close with Masaryk and Benes.

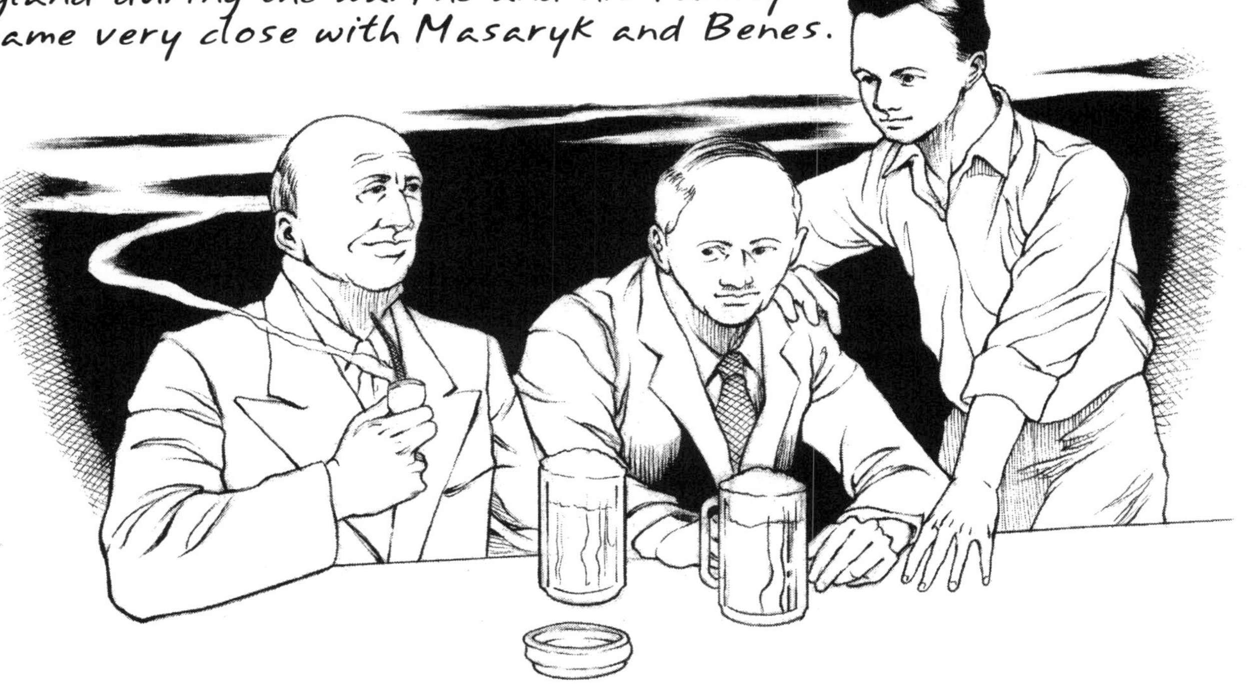

President Benes was the godfather of Josef's son Josef, Jr. and Jan Masaryk was the godfather my brother's other son, Vaclav. I know my brother valued his friendship with both men very much.

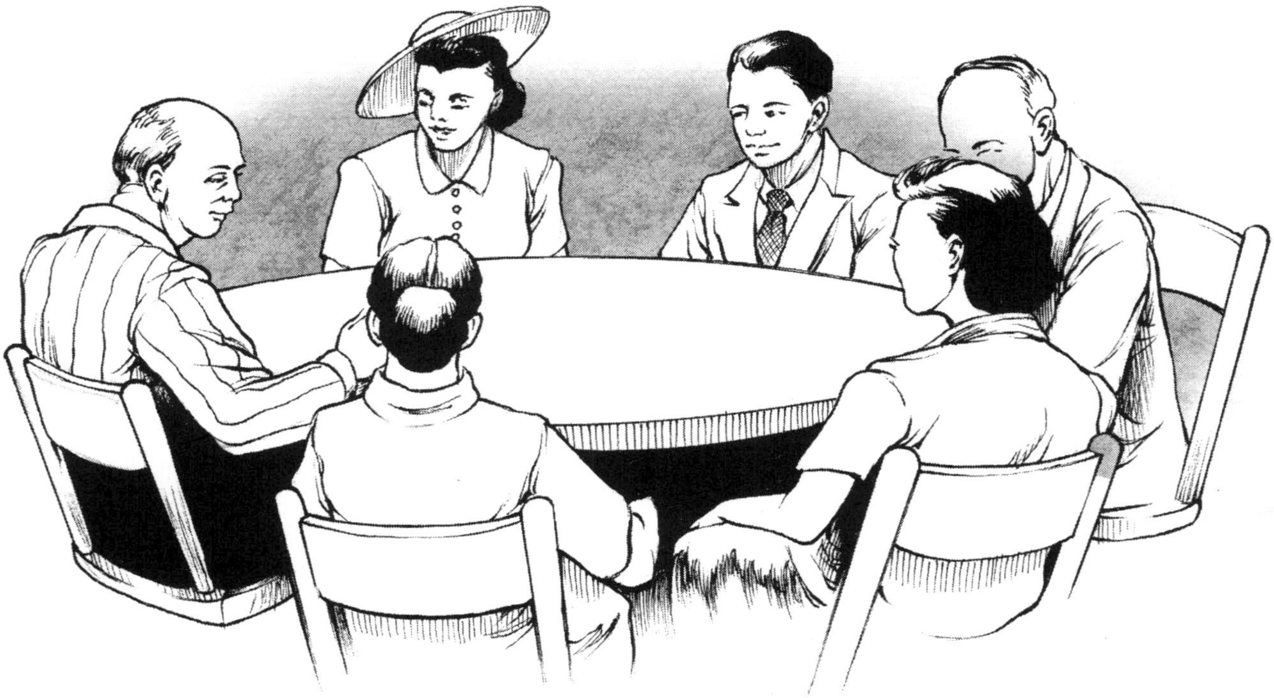

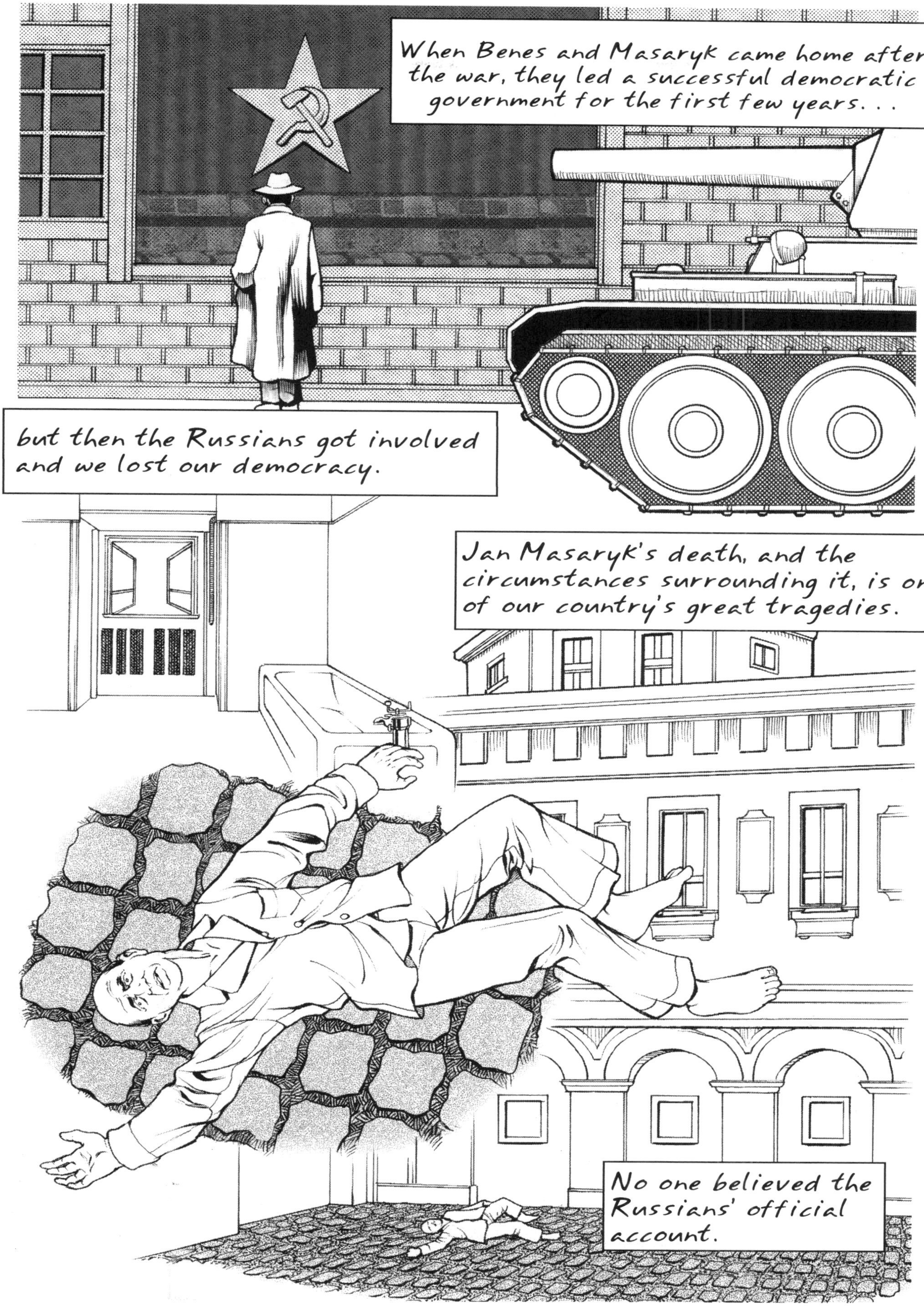
When Benes and Masaryk came home after the war, they led a successful democratic government for the first few years. . .
but then the Russians got involved and we lost our democracy.
Jan Masaryk's death, and the circumstances surrounding it, is one of our country's great tragedies.
No one believed the Russians' official account.

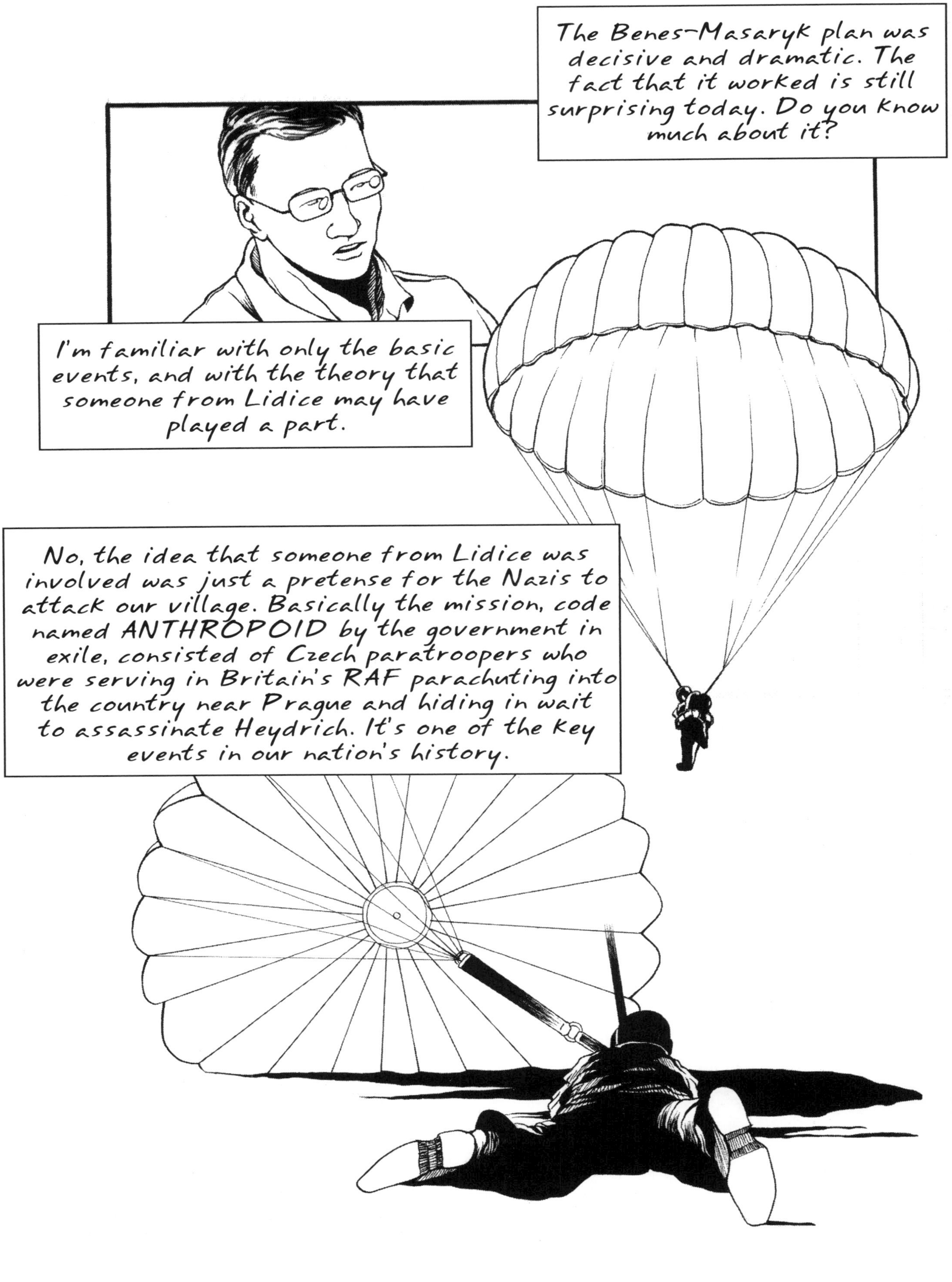
The Benes-Masaryk plan was decisive and dramatic. The fact that it worked is still surprising today. Do you know much about it?
I'm familiar with only the basic events, and with the theory that someone from Lidice may have played a part.
No, the idea that someone from Lidice was involved was just a pretense for the Nazis to attack our village. Basically the mission, code named ANTHROPOID by the government in exile, consisted of Czech paratroopers who were serving in Britain's RAF parachuting into the country near Prague and hiding in wait to assassinate Heydrich. It's one of the key events in our nation's history.

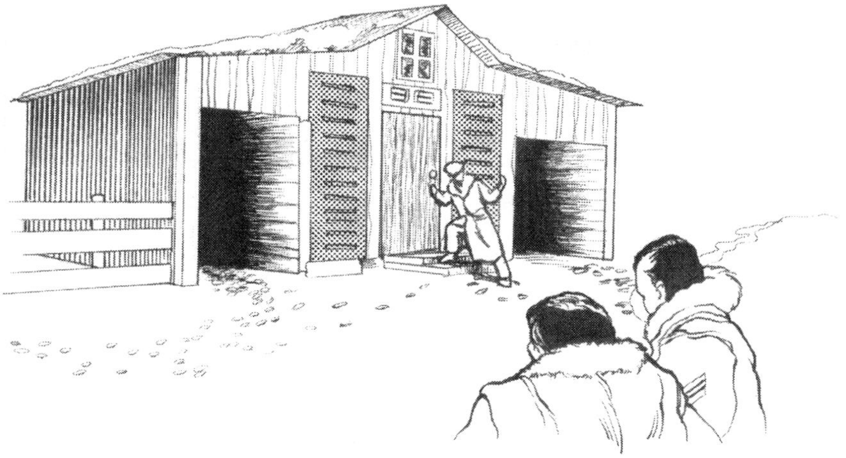

Heydrich's assassins, Josef Gabcik and Jan Kubis, dropped into Czechoslovakia in late December 1941, months before the attack. They were assisted in their preparations by Czech resistance fighters in Prague and Pilsen.

Finally a date for the attack was chosen May 27, 1942. This date was selected because the resistance movement learned that Heydrich was going to take a secret flight to attend a security conference with Hitler on that day. Their plan was to assassinate Heydrich and secure the important intelligence documents which he was sure to be transporting.

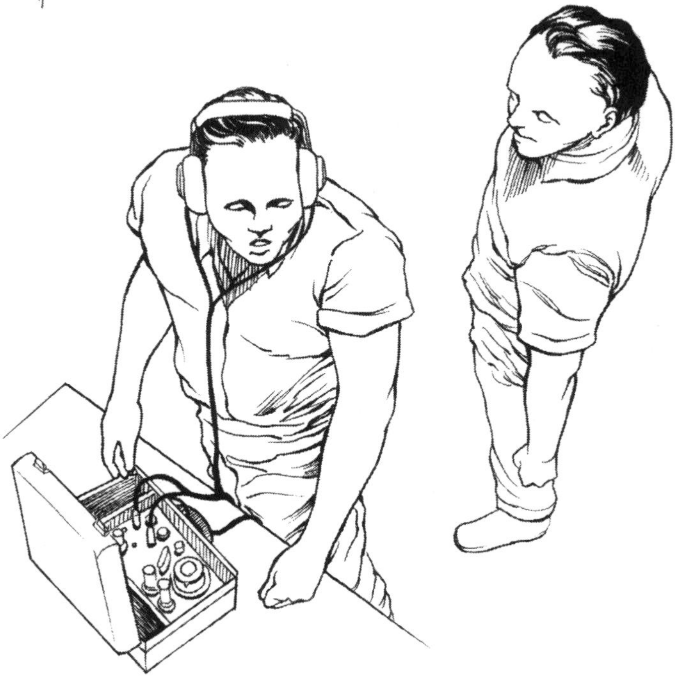

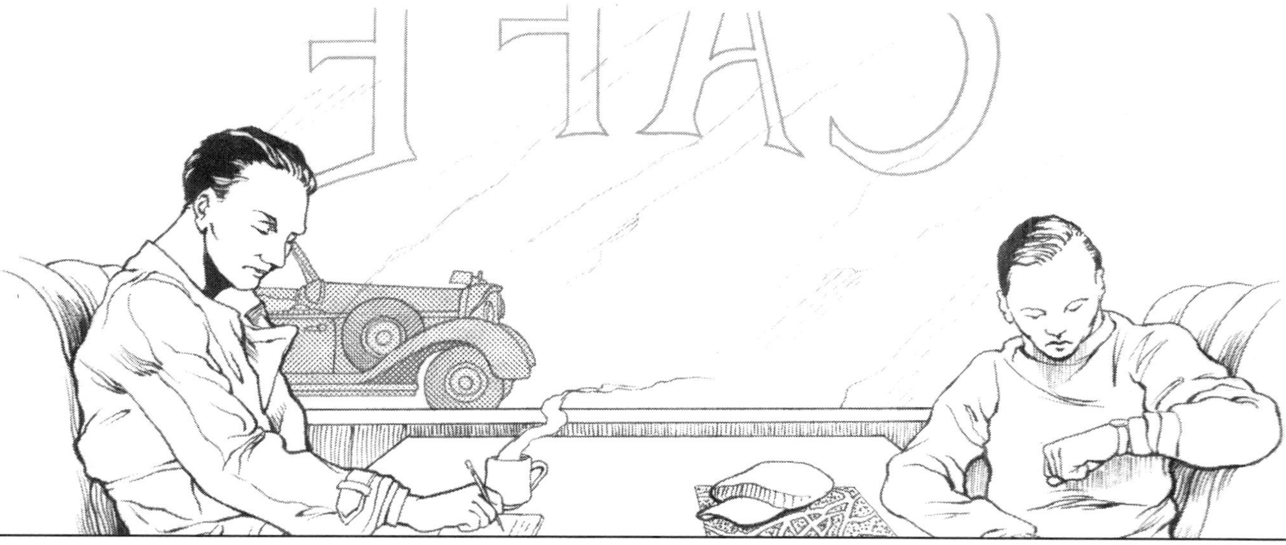

Kubis and Gabcik studied the route which Heydrich took to his office in the Prague Castle and found the point where it would be most vulnerable.

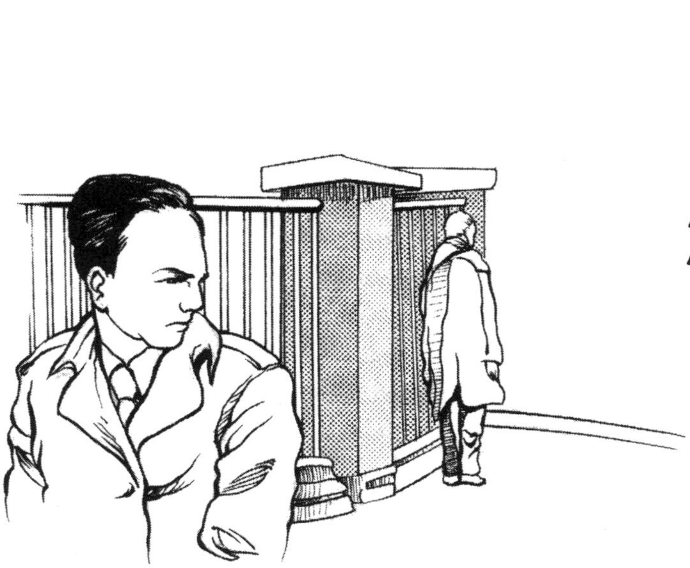

The trap was set. Josef Gabcik, posing as a worker riding his bicycle to work, was poised just before the bend in the road with a small, concealed sten gun. Jan Kubis, meanwhile, pretending to be on his way to catch a tram at the stop just around the curve, positioned himself with grenades to throw should his partner be unsuccessful.

Both fortune and misfortune visited the assassins that day. Luck was with them, for Heydrich was running late that morning and decided to forgo traveling with his security detail as it would slow him down. Therefore, Kubis and Gabcik had only the lone black Mercedes to deal with.

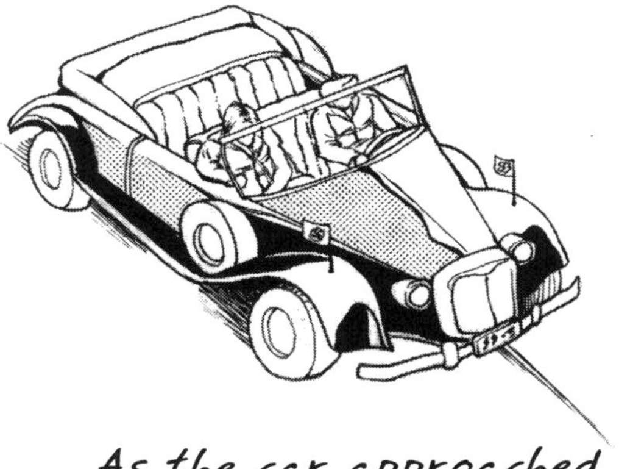

As the car approached Gabcik's position, he ran into the street and tried to fire his rifle. Unfortunately it jammed and he was unable to get off a single shot.

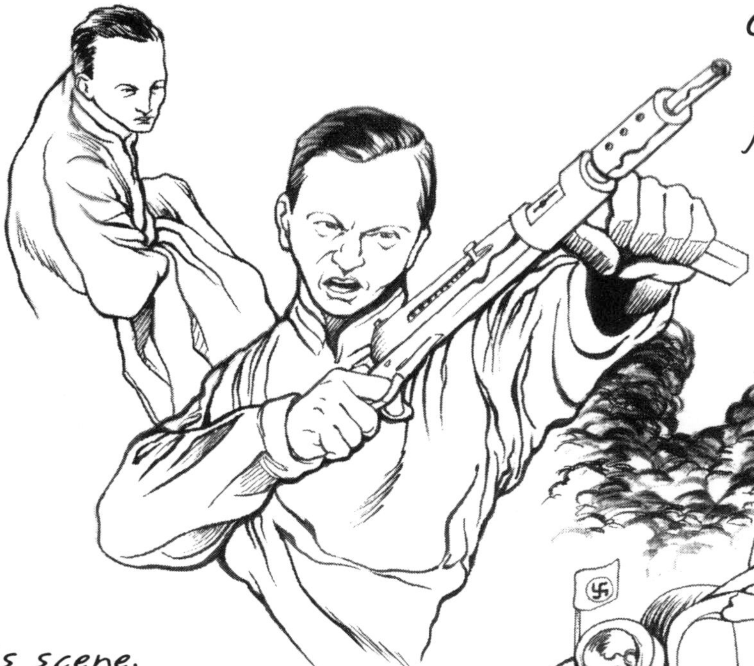

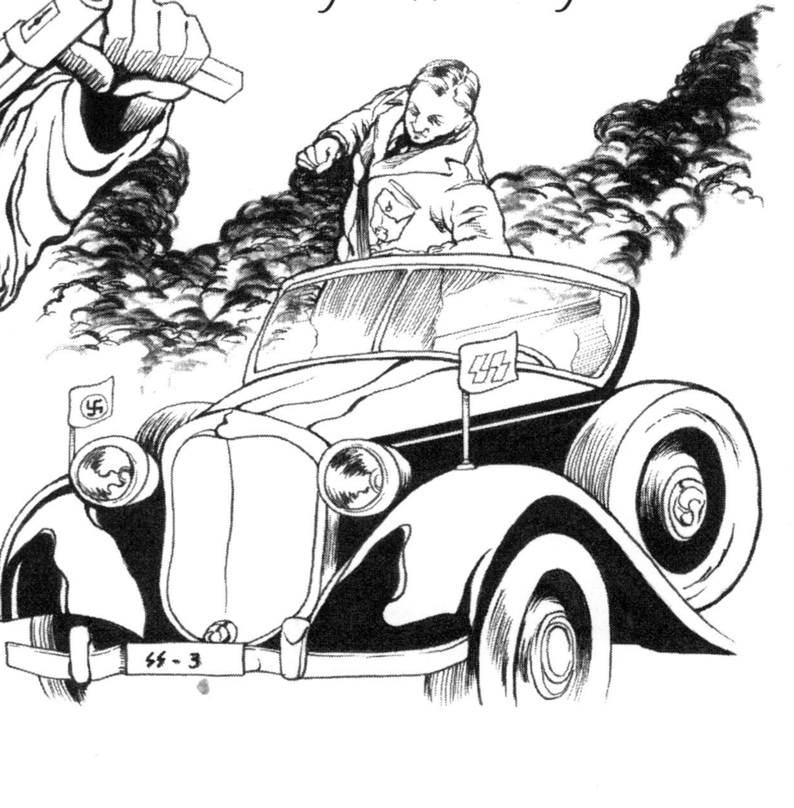
SS-3

This scene, however, provided enough distraction for Kubis to accurately throw a grenade which disabled the car and injured Reichsprotektor Heydrich.

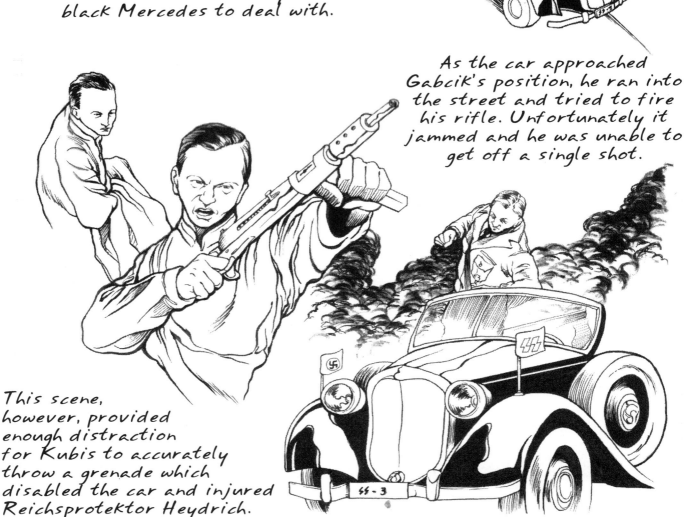

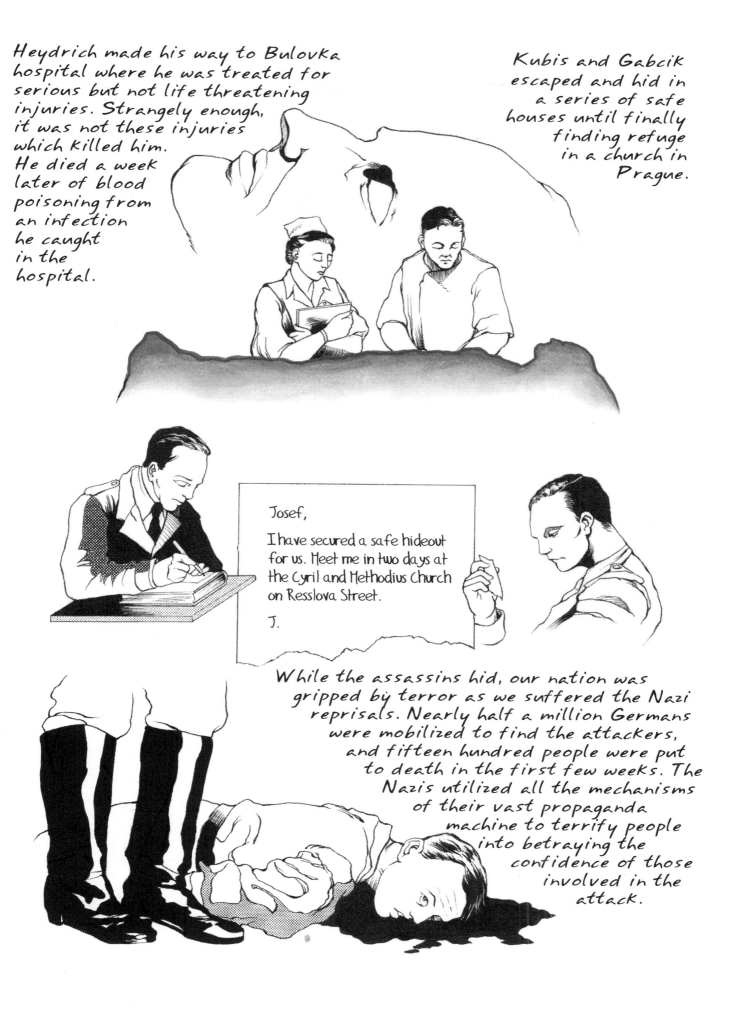

Heydrich made his way to Bulovka hospital where he was treated for serious but not life threatening injuries. Strangely enough, it was not these injuries which killed him. He died a week later of blood poisoning from an infection he caught in the hospital.

Kubis and Gabcik escaped and hid in a series of safe houses until finally finding refuge in a church in Prague.

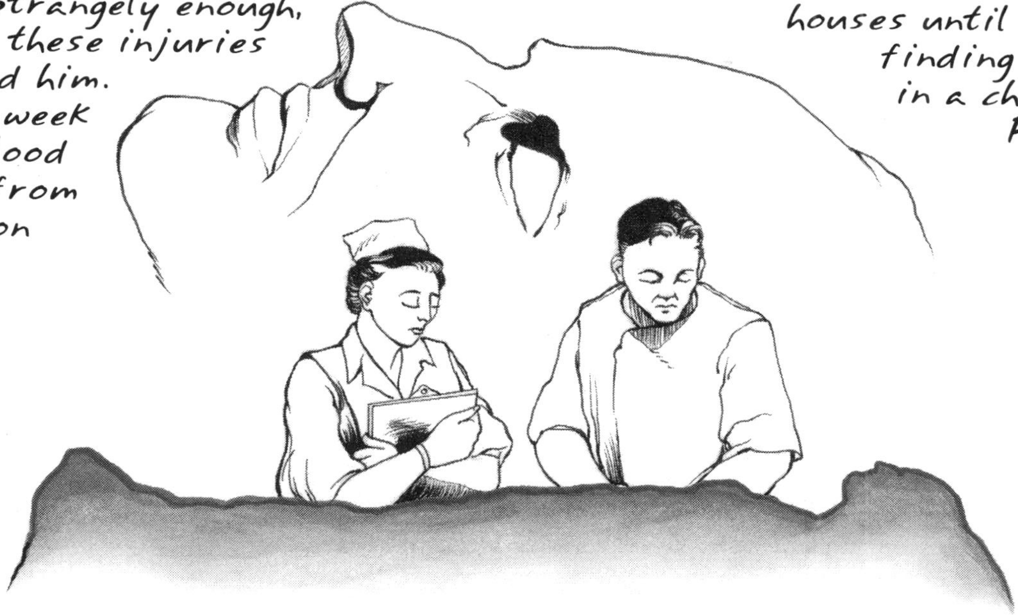

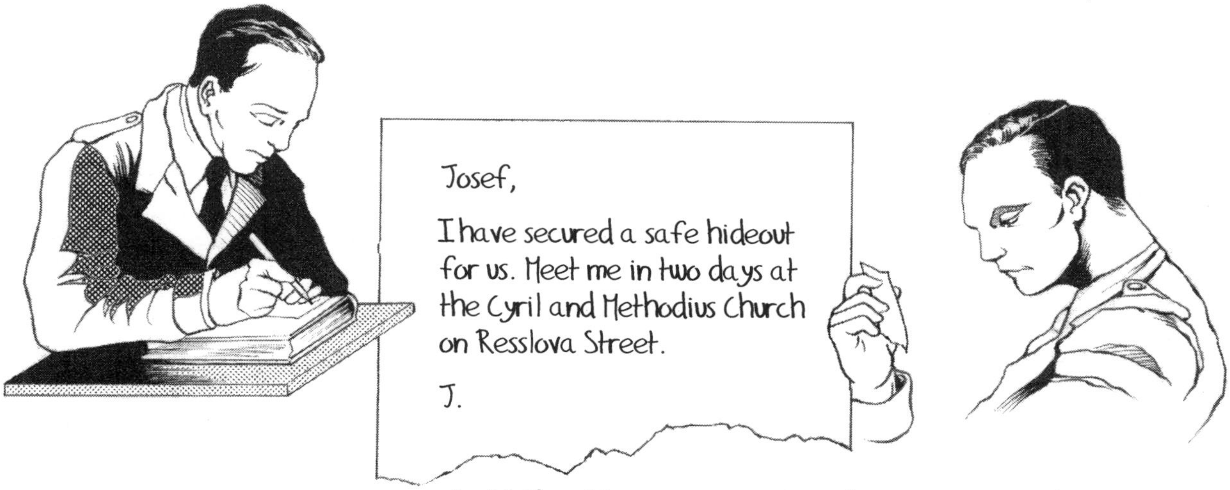
Josef,
I have secured a safe hideout for us. Meet me in two days at the Cyril and Methodius Church on Resslova Street.
J.

While the assassins hid, our nation was gripped by terror as we suffered the Nazi reprisals. Nearly half a million Germans were mobilized to find the attackers, and fifteen hundred people were put to death in the first few weeks. The Nazis utilized all the mechanisms of their vast propaganda machine to terrify people into betraying the confidence of those involved in the attack.

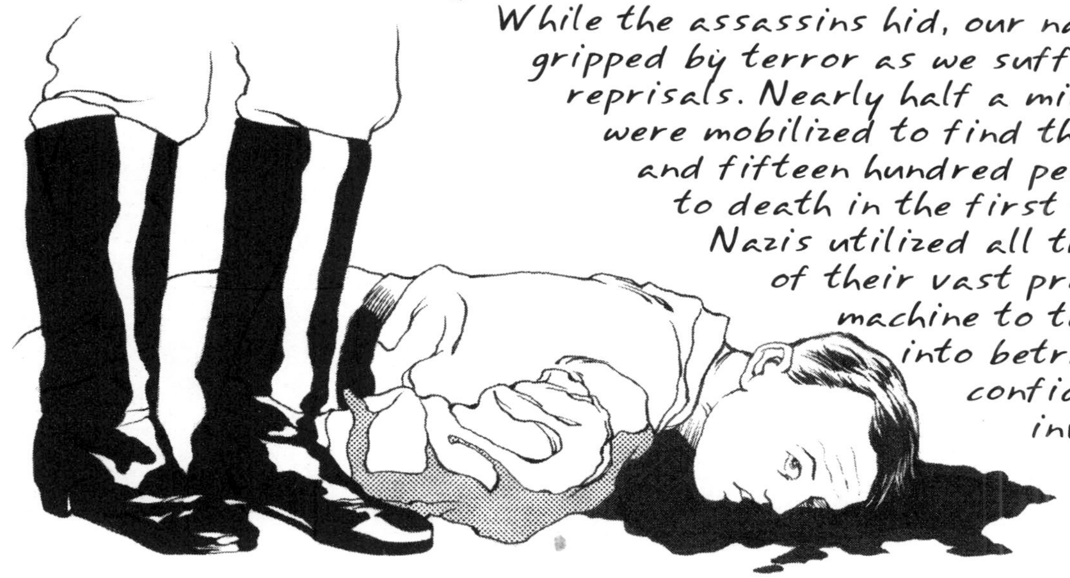

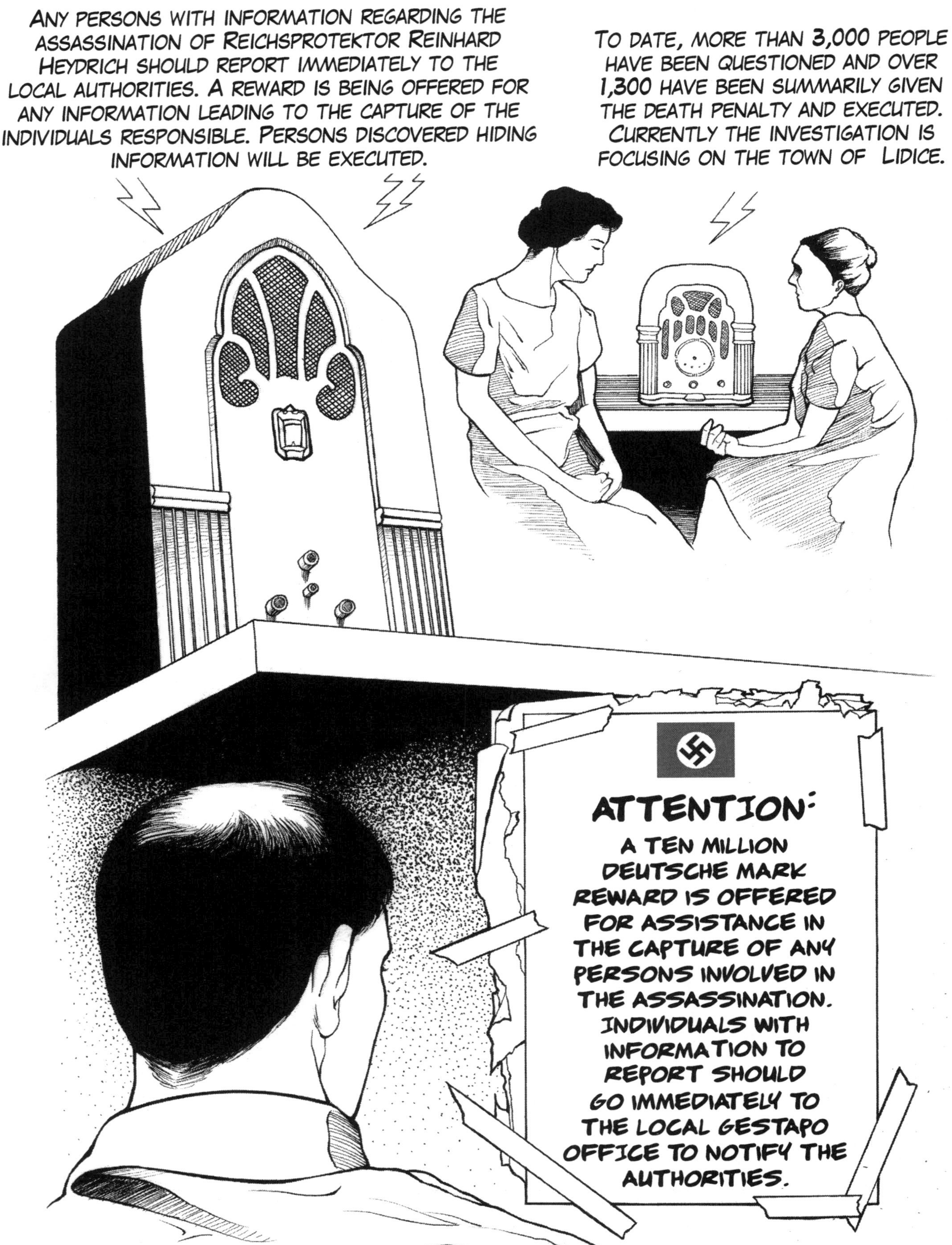
ANY PERSONS WITH INFORMATION REGARDING THE ASSASSINATION OF REICHSPROTEKTOR REINHARD HEYDRICH SHOULD REPORT IMMEDIATELY TO THE LOCAL AUTHORITIES. A REWARD IS BEING OFFERED FOR ANY INFORMATION LEADING TO THE CAPTURE OF THE INDIVIDUALS RESPONSIBLE. PERSONS DISCOVERED HIDING INFORMATION WILL BE EXECUTED.
TO DATE, MORE THAN 3,000 PEOPLE HAVE BEEN QUESTIONED AND OVER 1,300 HAVE BEEN SUMMARILY GIVEN THE DEATH PENALTY AND EXECUTED. CURRENTLY THE INVESTIGATION IS FOCUSING ON THE TOWN OF LIDICE.
ATTENTION:
A TEN MILLION DEUTSCHE MARK REWARD IS OFFERED FOR ASSISTANCE IN THE CAPTURE OF ANY PERSONS INVOLVED IN THE ASSASSINATION. INDIVIDUALS WITH INFORMATION TO REPORT SHOULD GO IMMEDIATELY TO THE LOCAL GESTAPO OFFICE TO NOTIFY THE AUTHORITIES.

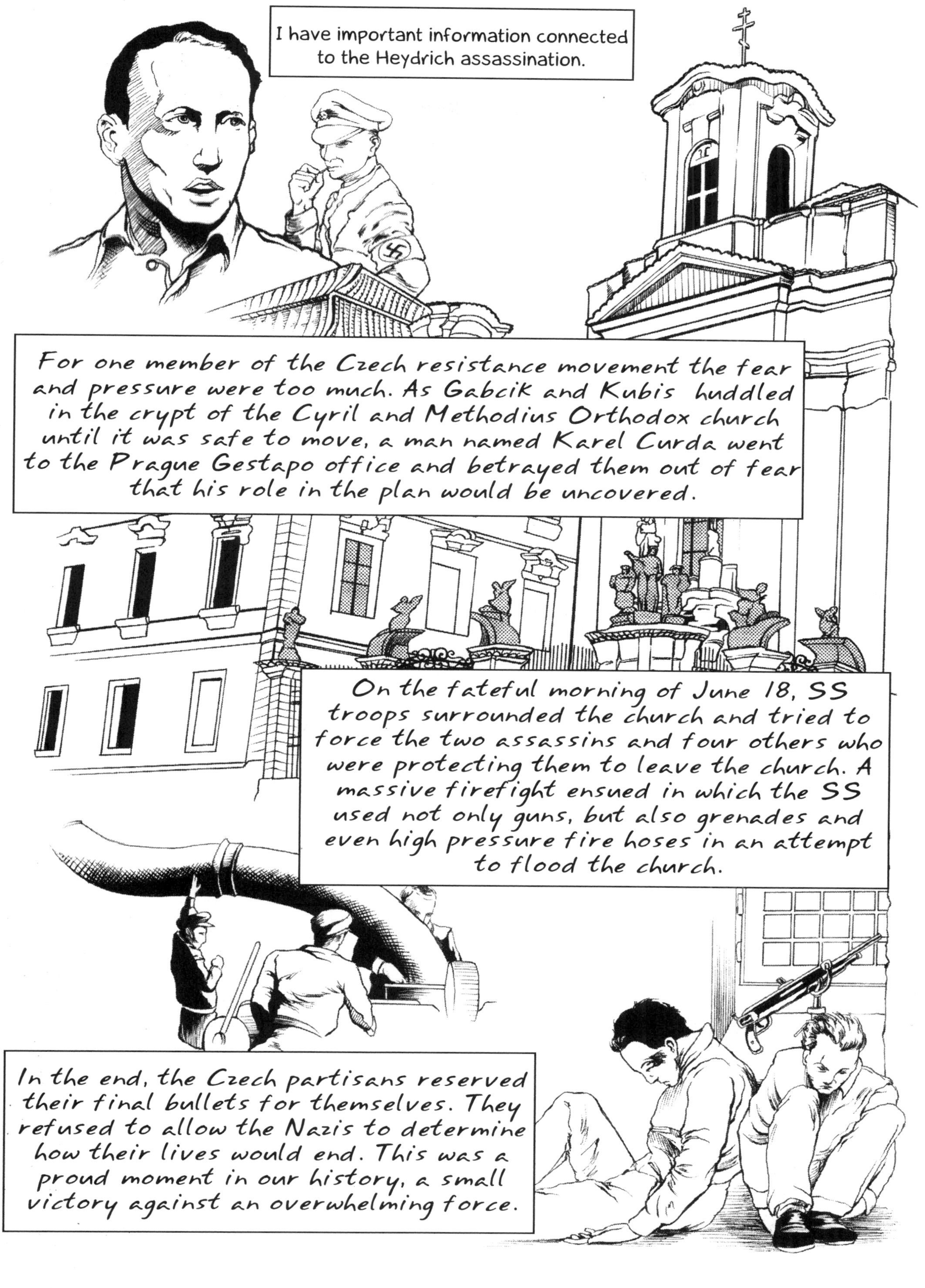
I have important information connected to the Heydrich assassination.
For one member of the Czech resistance movement the fear and pressure were too much. As Gabcik and Kubis huddled in the crypt of the Cyril and Methodius Orthodox church until it was safe to move, a man named Karel Curda went to the Prague Gestapo office and betrayed them out of fear that his role in the plan would be uncovered.
On the fateful morning of June 18, SS troops surrounded the church and tried to force the two assassins and four others who were protecting them to leave the church. A massive firefight ensued in which the SS used not only guns, but also grenades and even high pressure fire hoses in an attempt to flood the church.
In the end, the Czech partisans reserved their final bullets for themselves. They refused to allow the Nazis to determine how their lives would end. This was a proud moment in our history, a small victory against an overwhelming force.

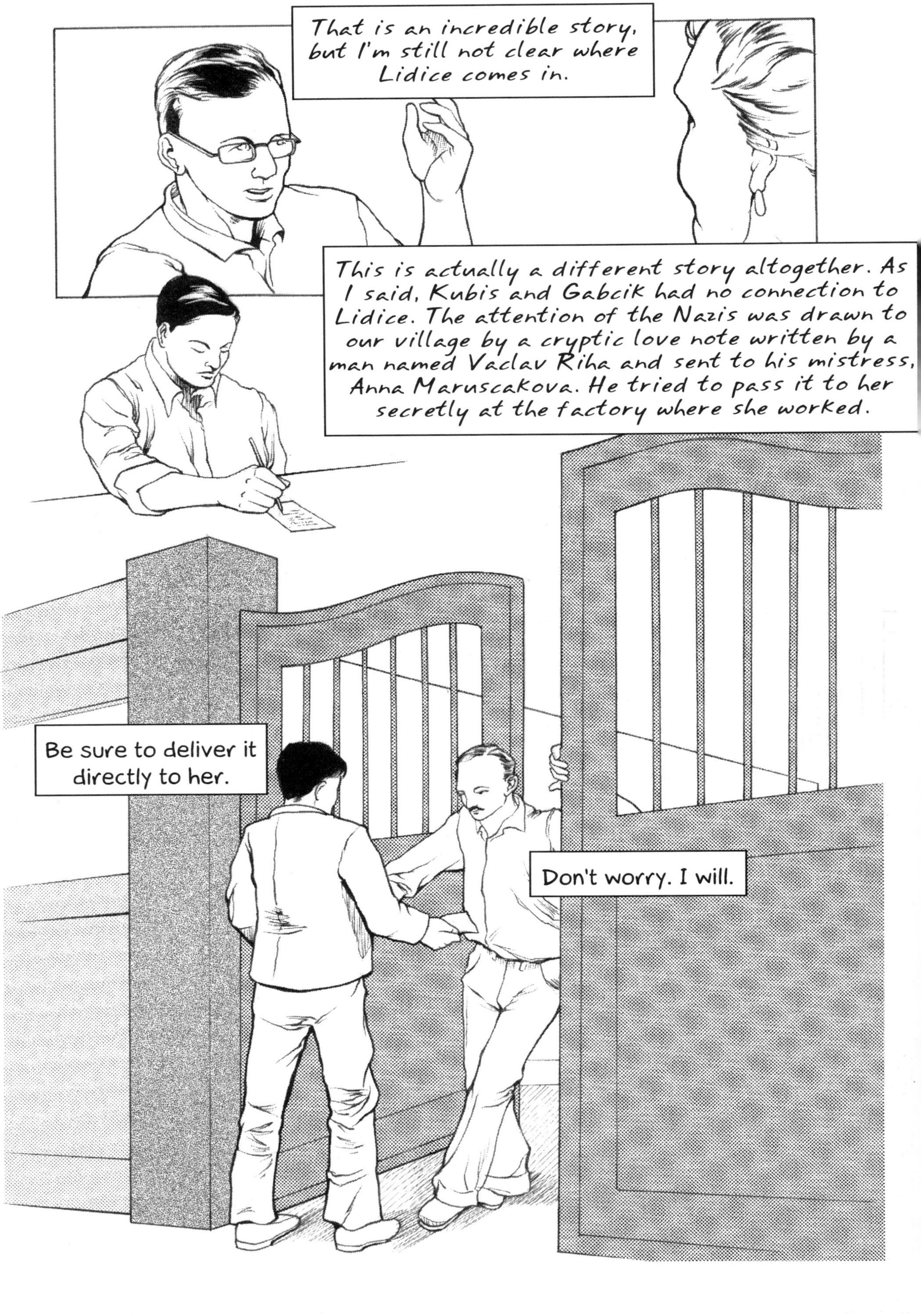
That is an incredible story, but I'm still not clear where Lidice comes in.
This is actually a different story altogether. As I said, Kubis and Gabcik had no connection to Lidice. The attention of the Nazis was drawn to our village by a cryptic love note written by a man named Vaclav Riha and sent to his mistress, Anna Maruscakova. He tried to pass it to her secretly at the factory where she worked.
Be sure to deliver it directly to her.
Don't worry. I will.

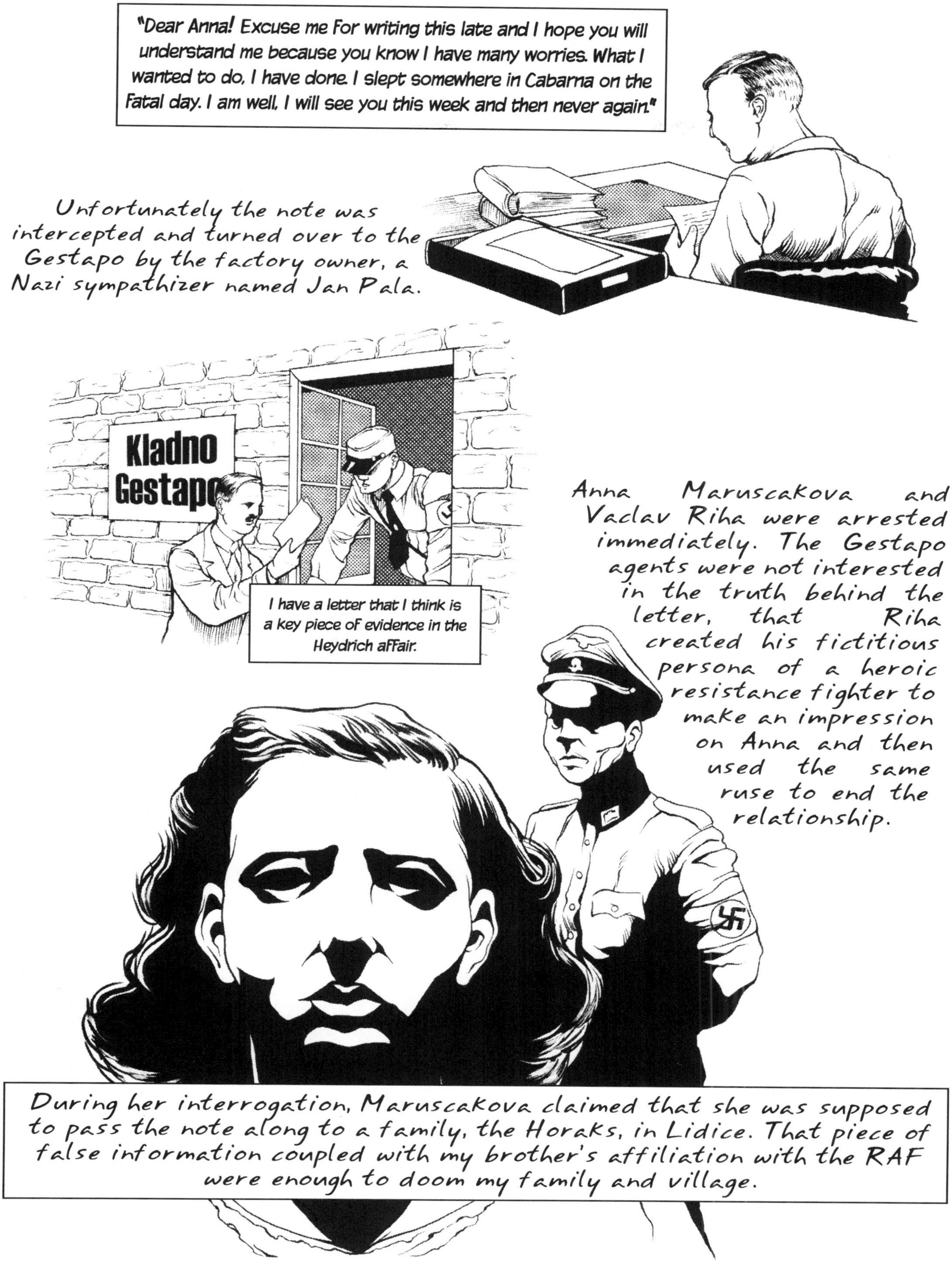
"Dear Anna! Excuse me For writing this late and I hope you will understand me because you know I have many worries. What I wanted to do, I have done. I slept somewhere in Cabarna on the Fatal day. I am well, I will see you this week and then never again."
Unfortunately the note was intercepted and turned over to the Gestapo by the factory owner, a Nazi sympathizer named Jan Pala.
Kladno Gestapo
I have a letter that I think is a key piece of evidence in the Heydrich aFFair.
Anna Maruscakova and Vaclav Riha were arrested immediately. The Gestapo agents were not interested in the truth behind the letter, that Riha created his fictitious persona of a heroic resistance fighter to make an impression on Anna and then used the same ruse to end the relationship.
During her interrogation, Maruscakova claimed that she was supposed to pass the note along to a family, the Horaks, in Lidice. That piece of false information coupled with my brother's affiliation with the RAF were enough to doom my family and village.

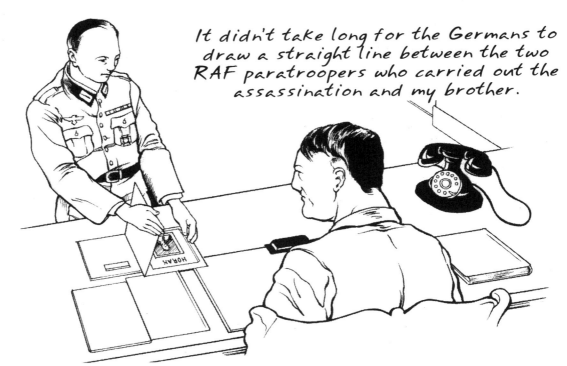

It didn't take long for the Germans to draw a straight line between the two RAF paratroopers who carried out the assassination and my brother.

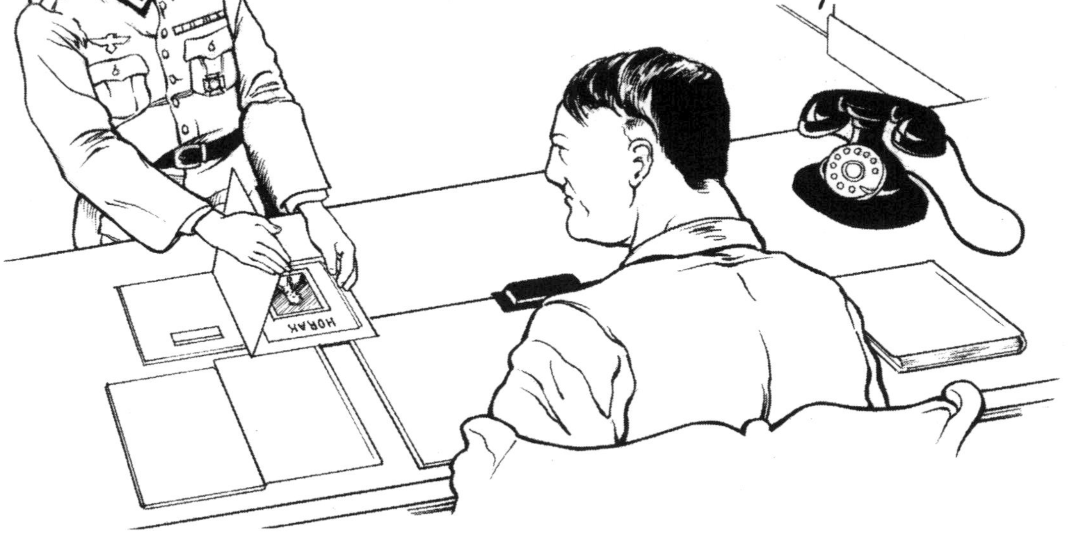
HORAK

They began drawing up plans immediately. There was of course no connection. It was later shown the Germans were aware of this...

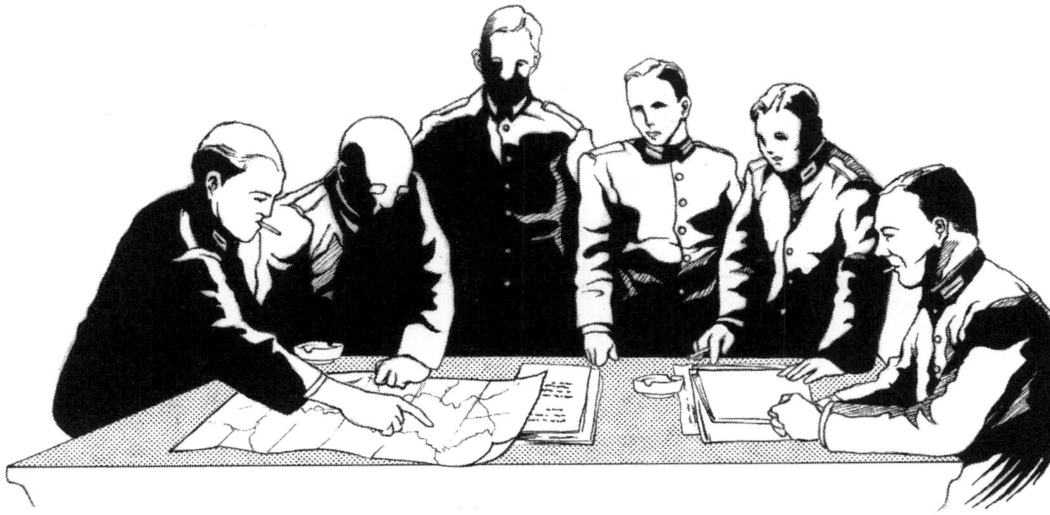

...it made no difference to them. They needed an example for the world to see. My family and my village were to be that example.

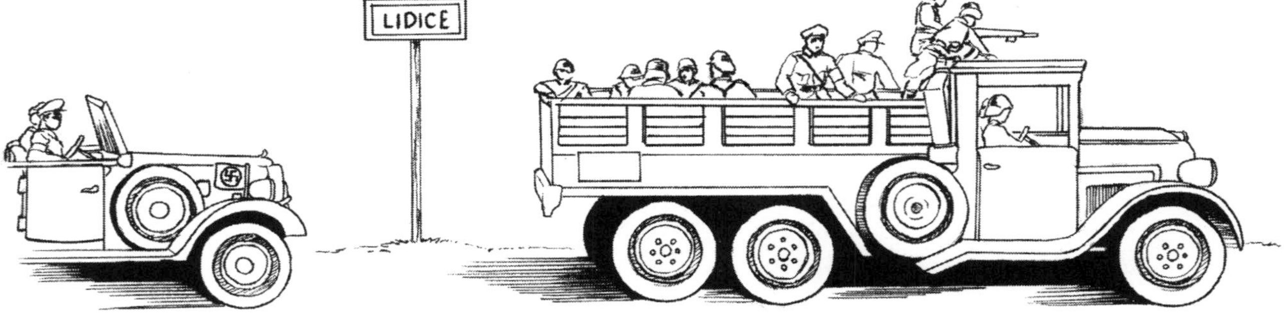
LIDICE

The Germans descended on us at daybreak one morning in June. The calm summer morning did not portend what was coming to our village. They swept into our houses like a storm and interrogated us about Josef. Our answers were true but unsatisfying to them.

I swear I haven't seen him ...   since he left for work ...   one morning over two years ago...   that's all I know.

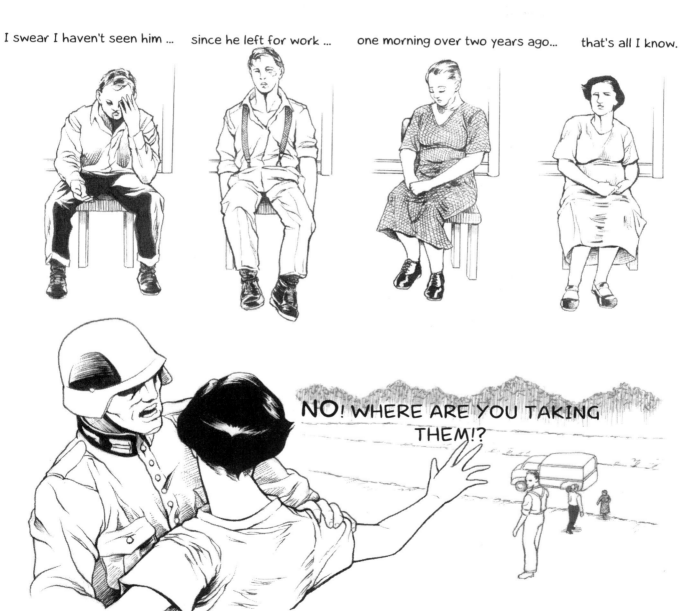

NO! WHERE ARE YOU TAKING THEM!?

My husband, parents, and all my relatives were led away. In total fifteen people from my family were taken from me that day. Aunts, uncles, everyone.

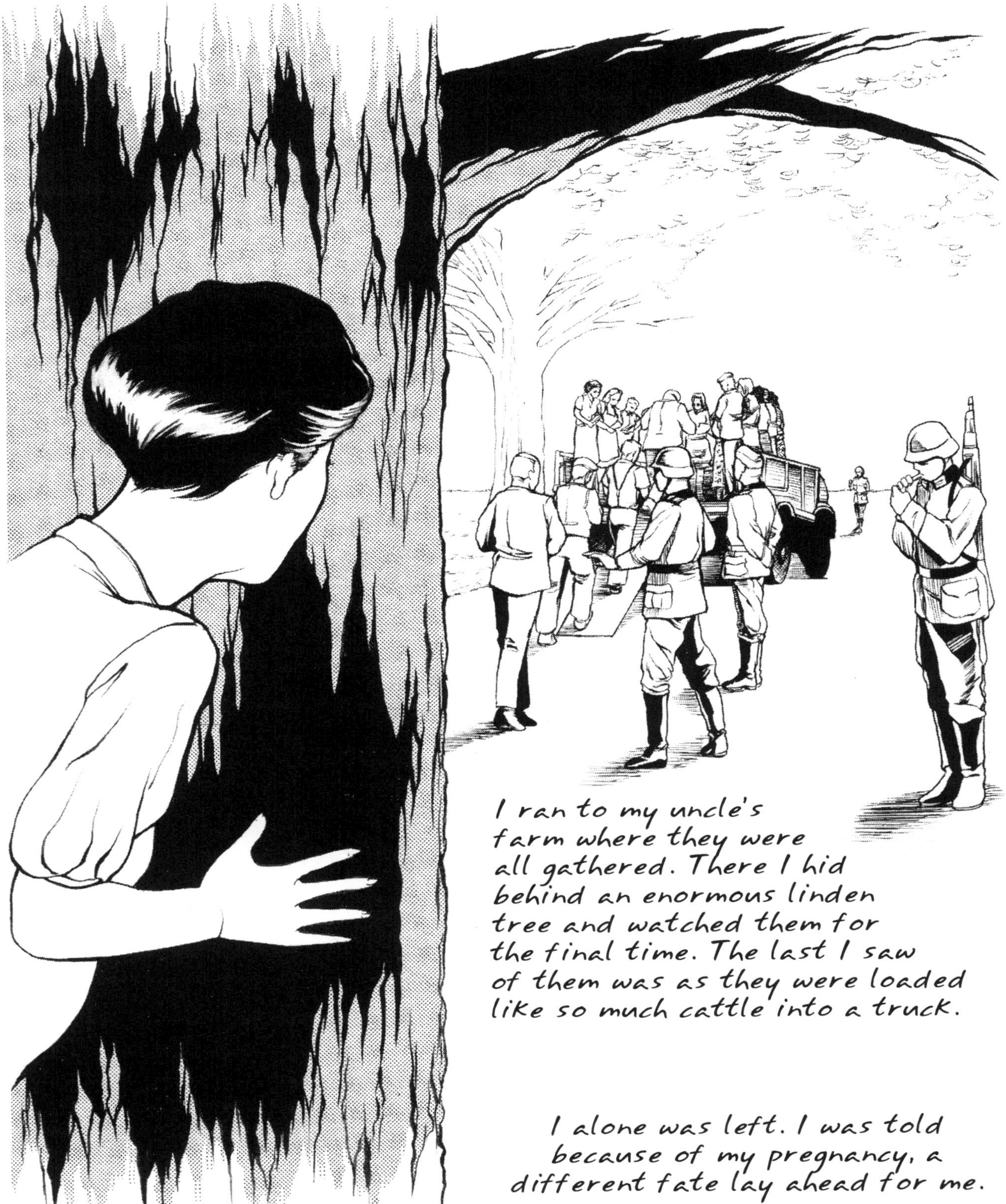
I ran to my uncle's farm where they were all gathered. There I hid behind an enormous linden tree and watched them for the final time. The last I saw of them was as they were loaded like so much cattle into a truck.
I alone was left. I was told because of my pregnancy, a different fate lay ahead for me.

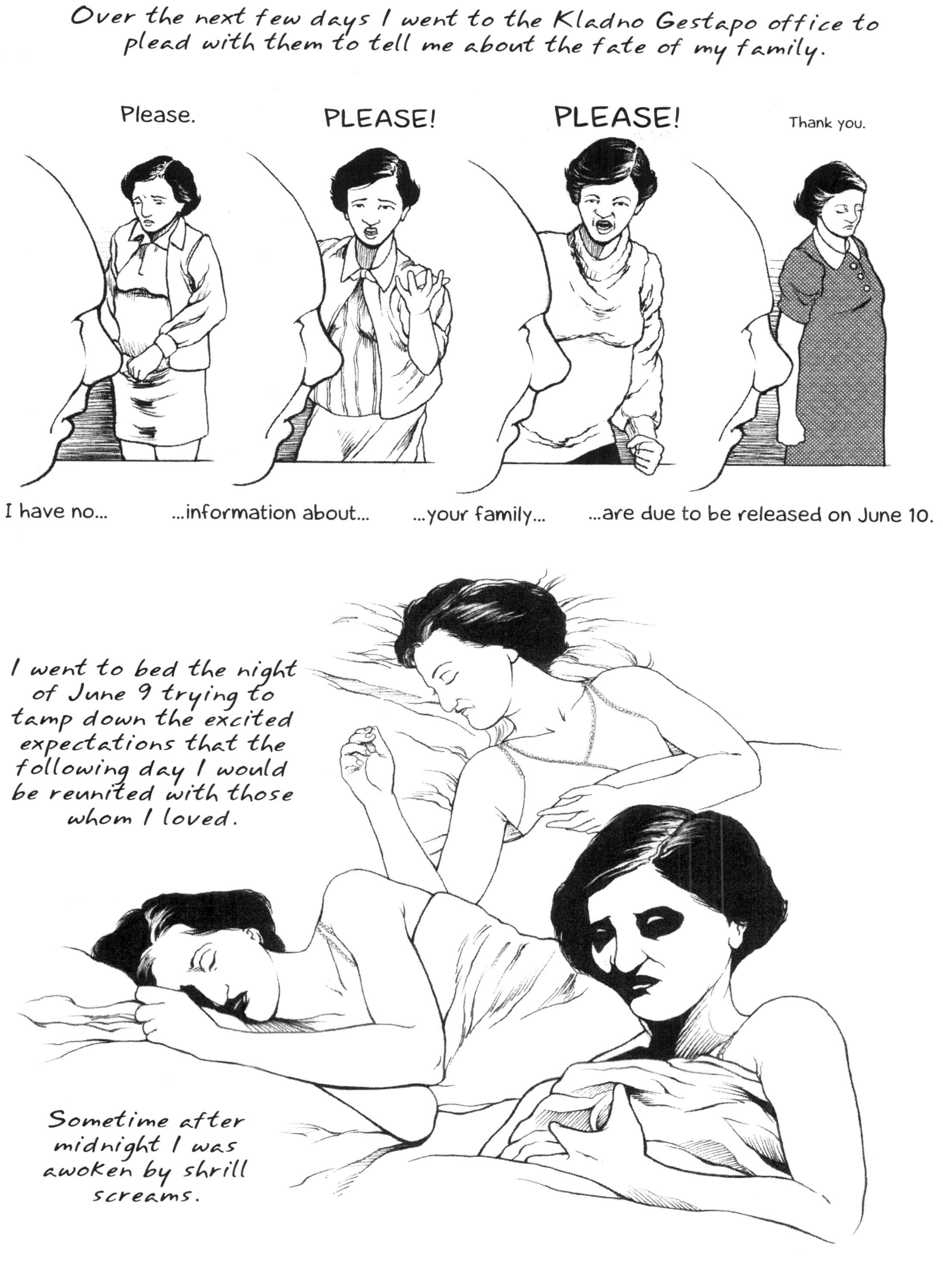

Over the next few days I went to the Kladno Gestapo office to plead with them to tell me about the fate of my family.
Please.
I have no...
PLEASE!
...information about...
PLEASE!
...your family...
Thank you.
...are due to be released on June 10.
I went to bed the night of June 9 trying to tamp down the excited expectations that the following day I would be reunited with those whom I loved.
Sometime after midnight I was awoken by shrill screams.

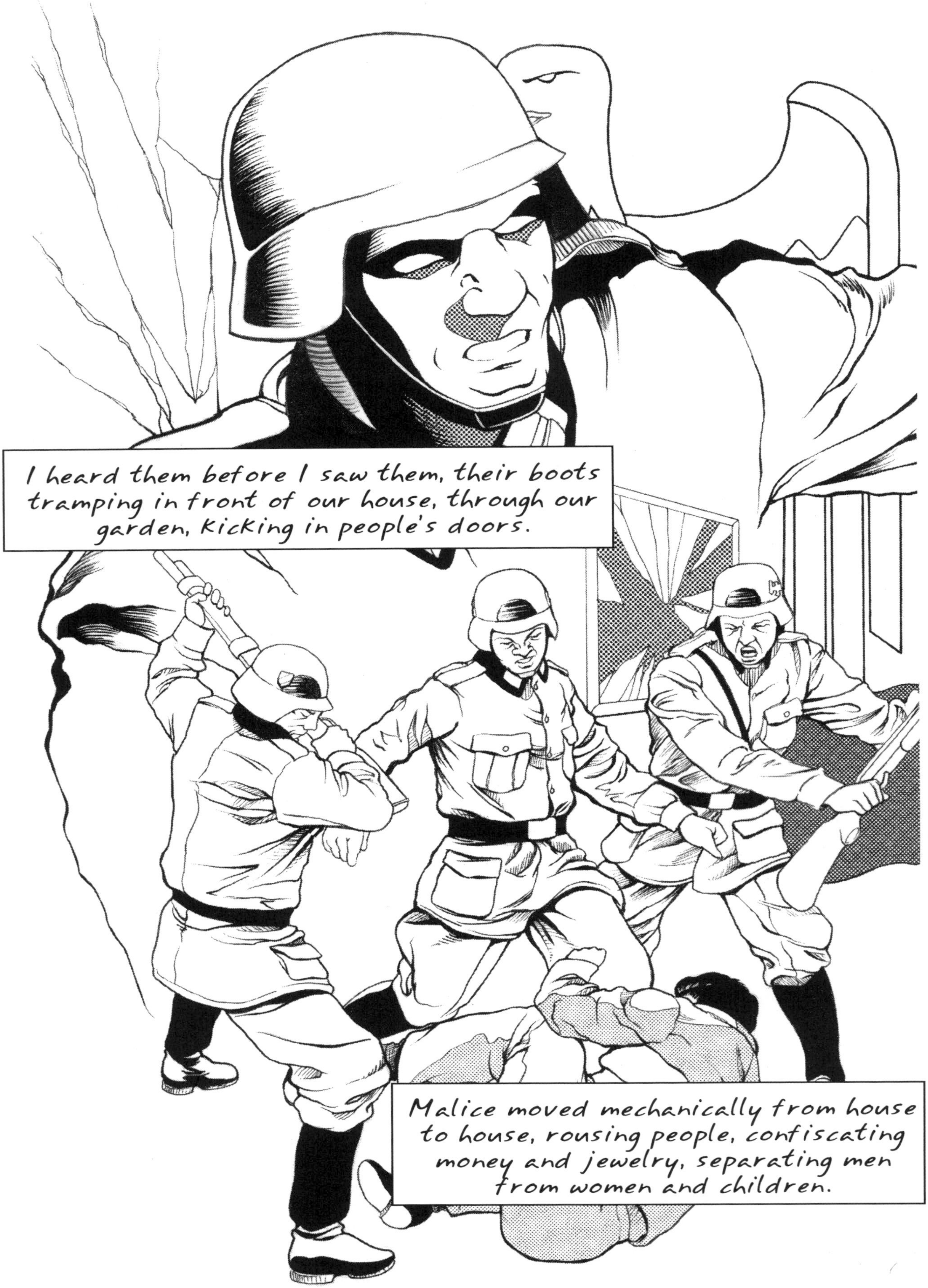
I heard them before I saw them, their boots tramping in front of our house, through our garden, kicking in people's doors.
Malice moved mechanically from house to house, rousing people, confiscating money and jewelry, separating men from women and children.

When they finally came to my door, the candle that I huddled with in the corner of the room was nearly extinguished by the rush of air into the room as the door burst open.

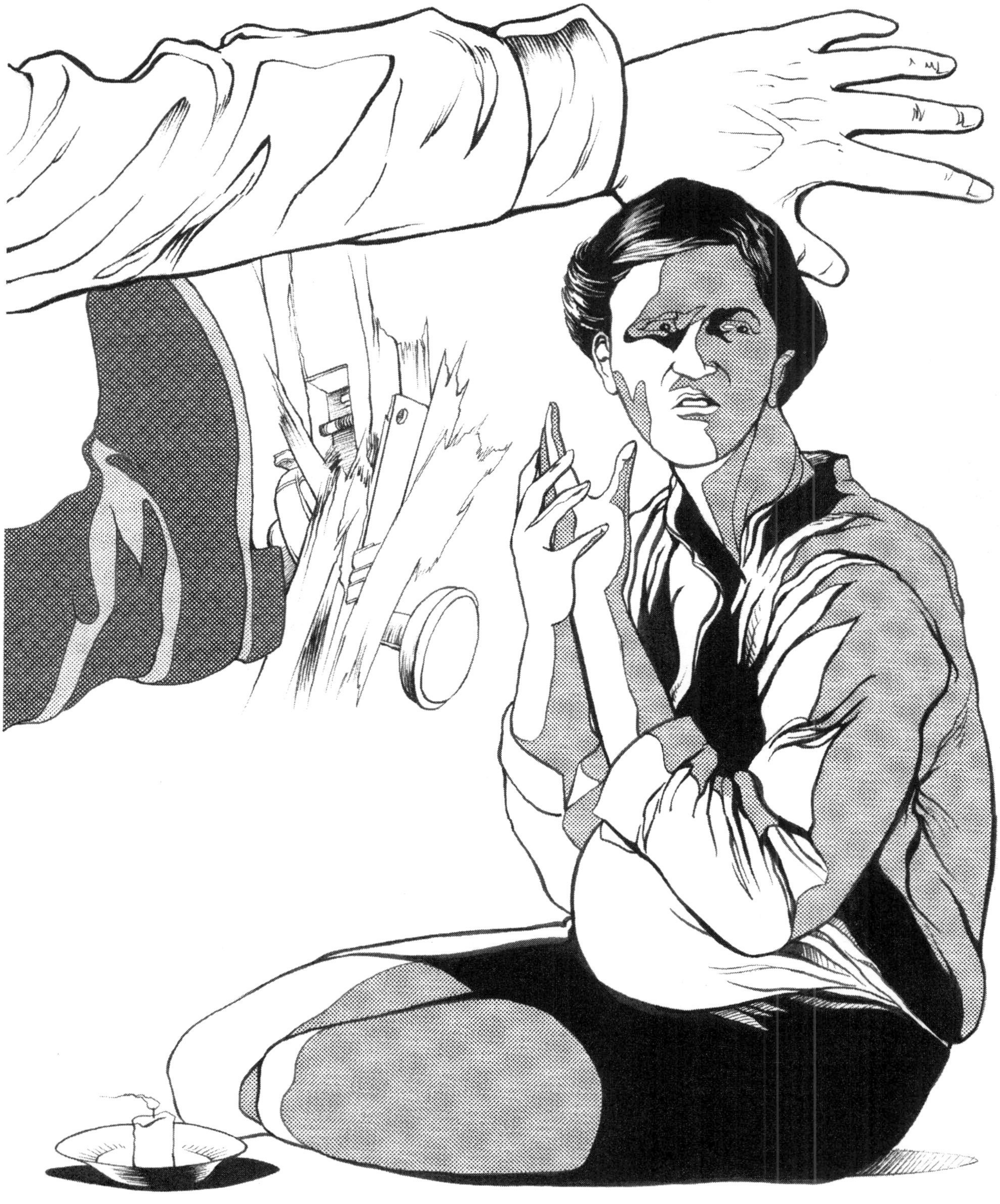

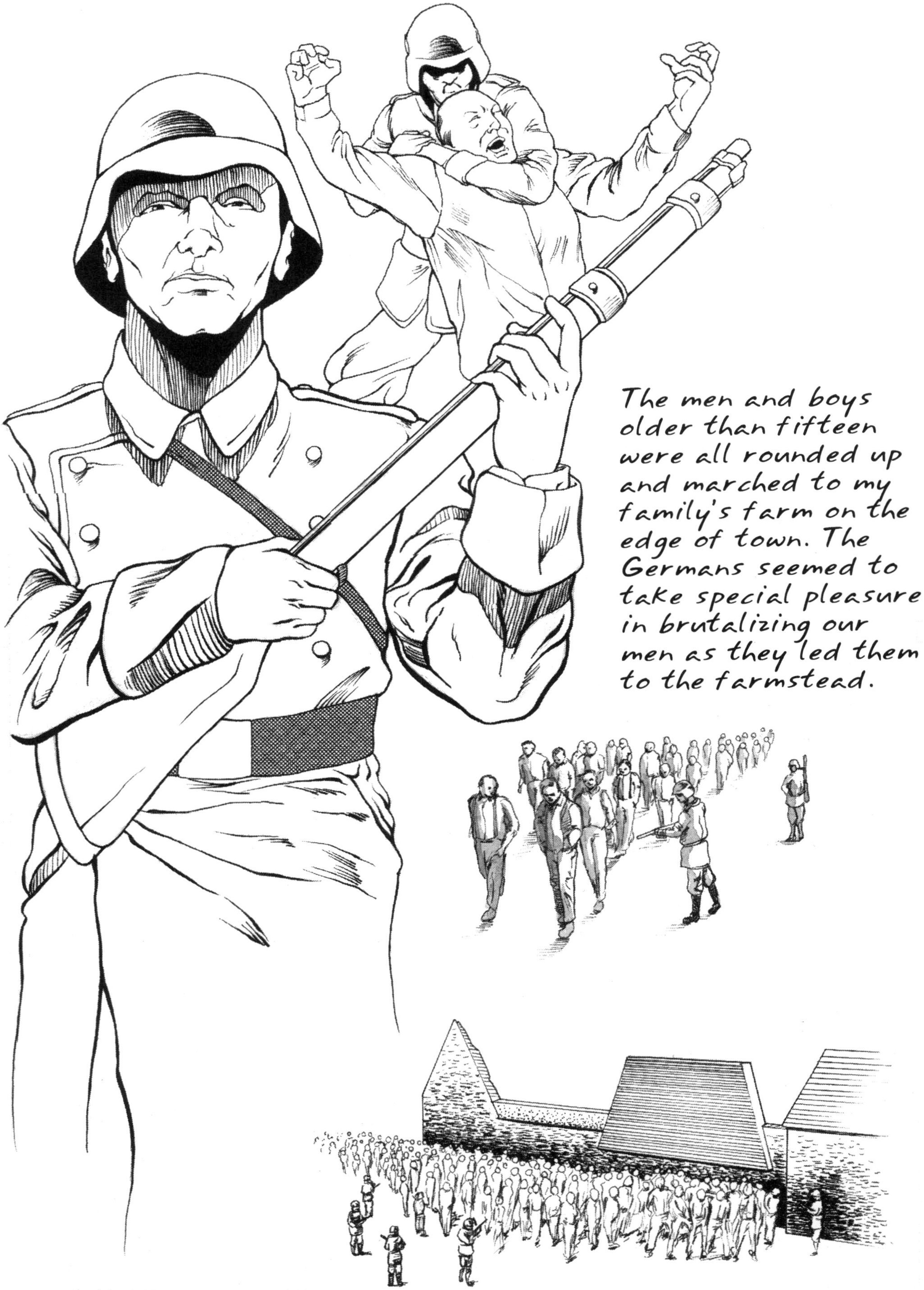
The men and boys older than fifteen were all rounded up and marched to my family's farm on the edge of town. The Germans seemed to take special pleasure in brutalizing our men as they led them to the farmstead.

We, the women and children, were separated from the men and loaded into open trucks. We were forced to leave with only five plums, which means as you say, "with just the shirt on your back."

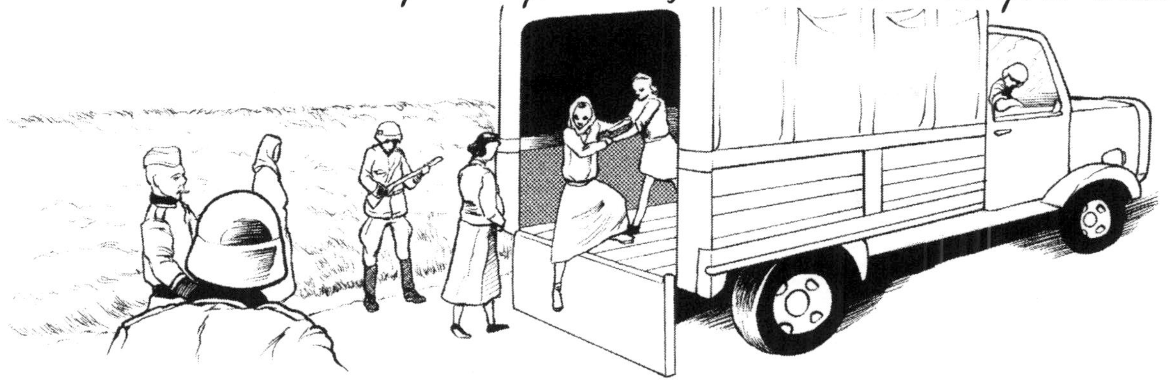

I was terrified, confused, hysterical. On our way out of town we passed a pasture on my family's farm where geese always gathered. Children loved to go to this field to chase the geese.

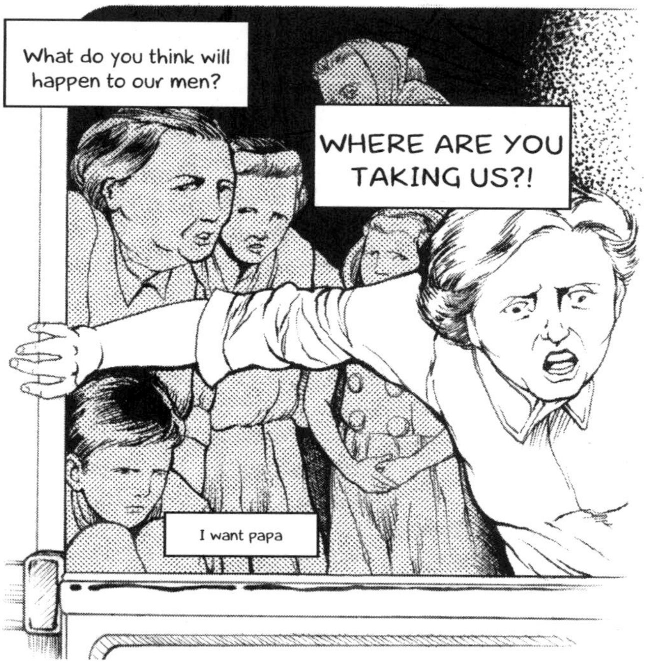
What do you think will happen to our men?
WHERE ARE YOU TAKING US?!
I want papa

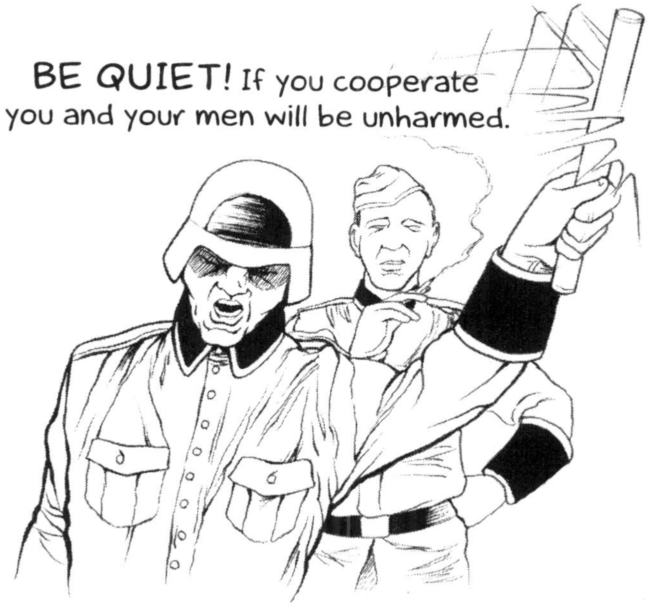
BE QUIET! If you cooperate you and your men will be unharmed.

Now as we were driven away to a nearby secondary school, gathered in this very same pasture we saw our fathers, husbands, brothers, and sons for the last time.

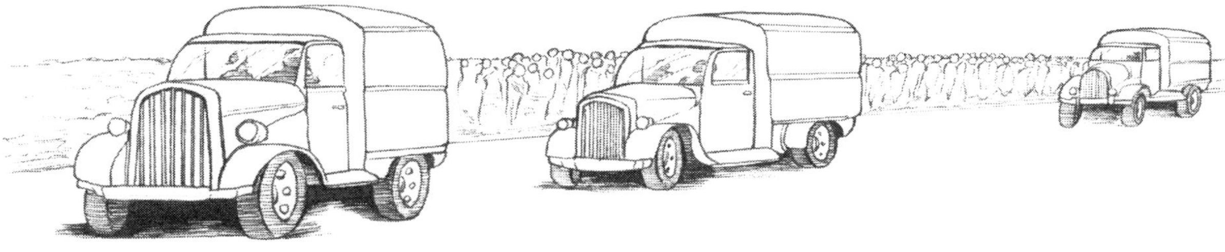

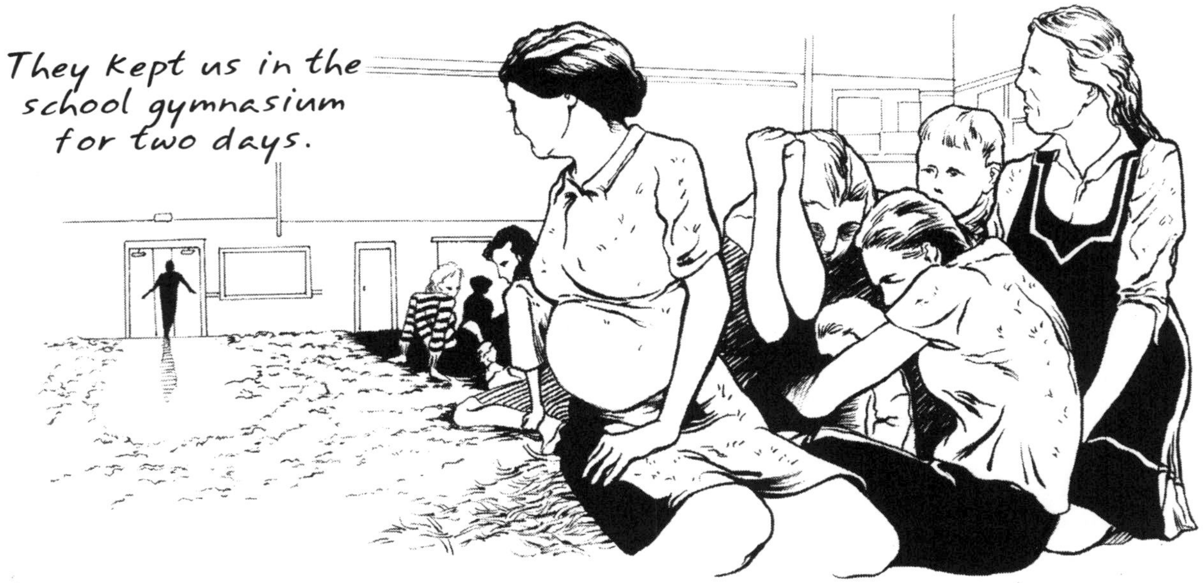
They kept us in the school gymnasium for two days.

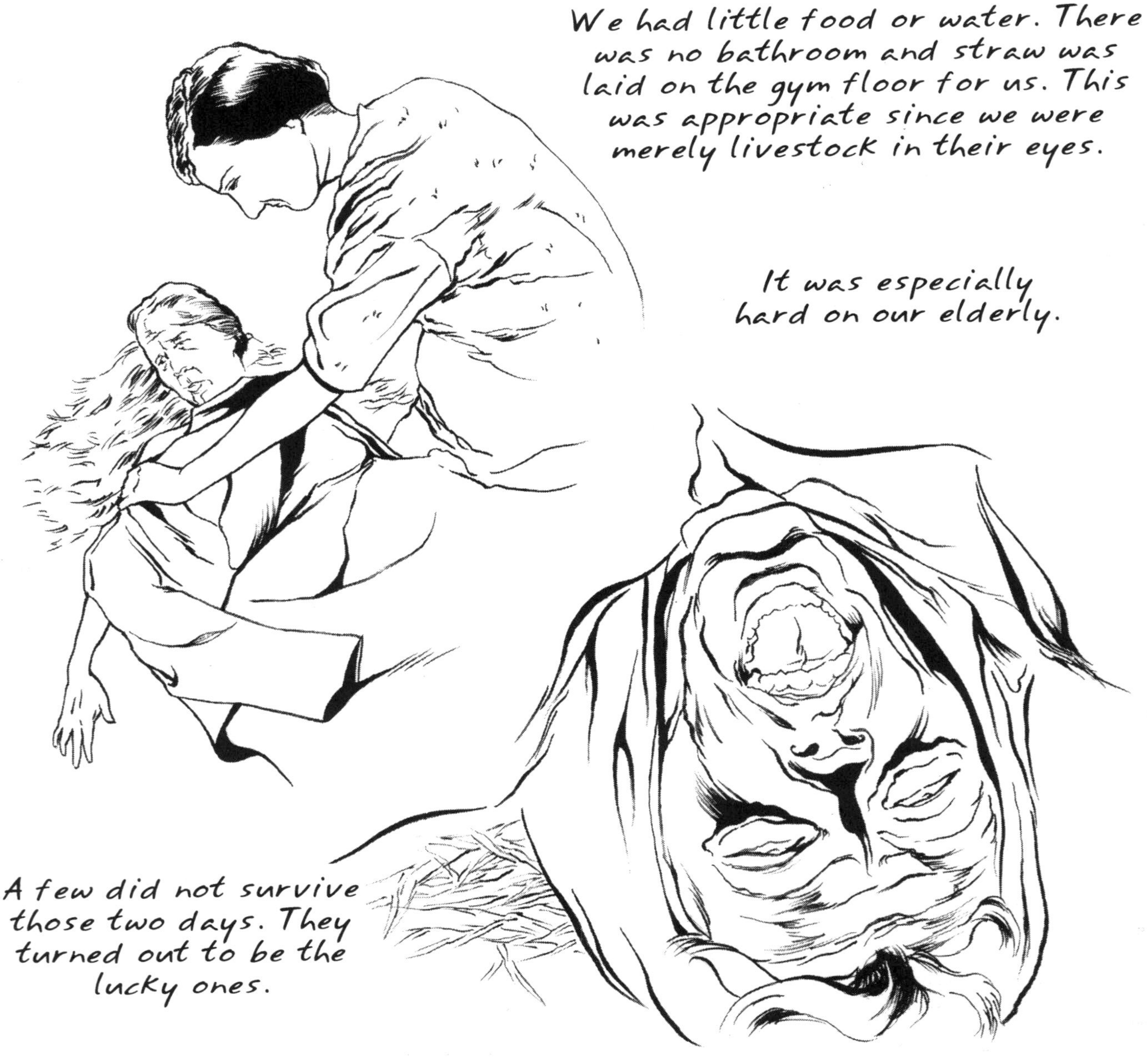
We had little food or water. There was no bathroom and straw was laid on the gym floor for us. This was appropriate since we were merely livestock in their eyes.
It was especially hard on our elderly.
A few did not survive those two days. They turned out to be the lucky ones.

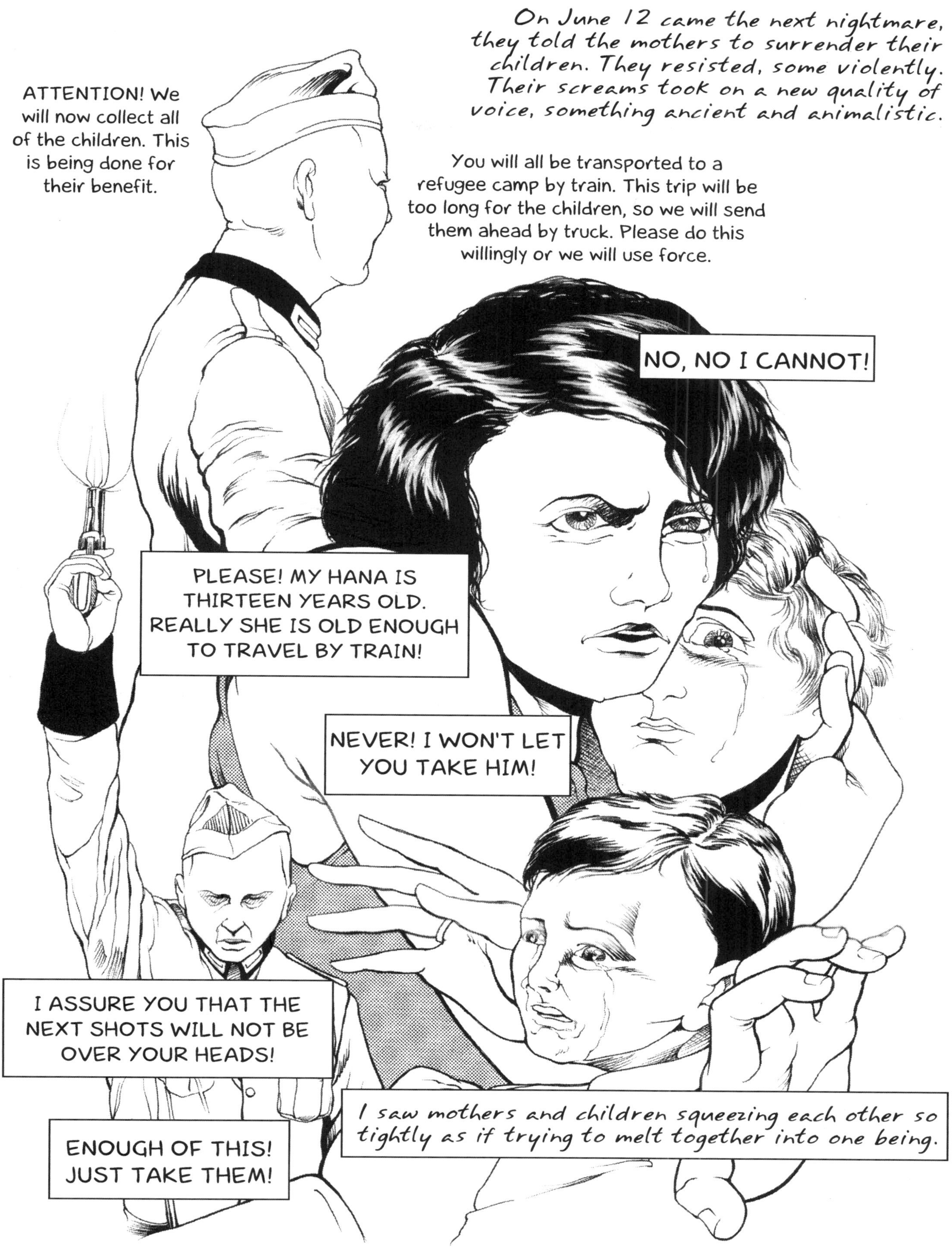
On June 12 came the next nightmare, they told the mothers to surrender their children. They resisted, some violently. Their screams took on a new quality of voice, something ancient and animalistic.
ATTENTION! We will now collect all of the children. This is being done for their benefit.
You will all be transported to a refugee camp by train. This trip will be too long for the children, so we will send them ahead by truck. Please do this willingly or we will use force.
NO, NO I CANNOT!
PLEASE! MY HANA IS THIRTEEN YEARS OLD. REALLY SHE IS OLD ENOUGH TO TRAVEL BY TRAIN!
NEVER! I WON'T LET YOU TAKE HIM!
I ASSURE YOU THAT THE NEXT SHOTS WILL NOT BE OVER YOUR HEADS!
ENOUGH OF THIS! JUST TAKE THEM!
I saw mothers and children squeezing each other so tightly as if trying to melt together into one being.

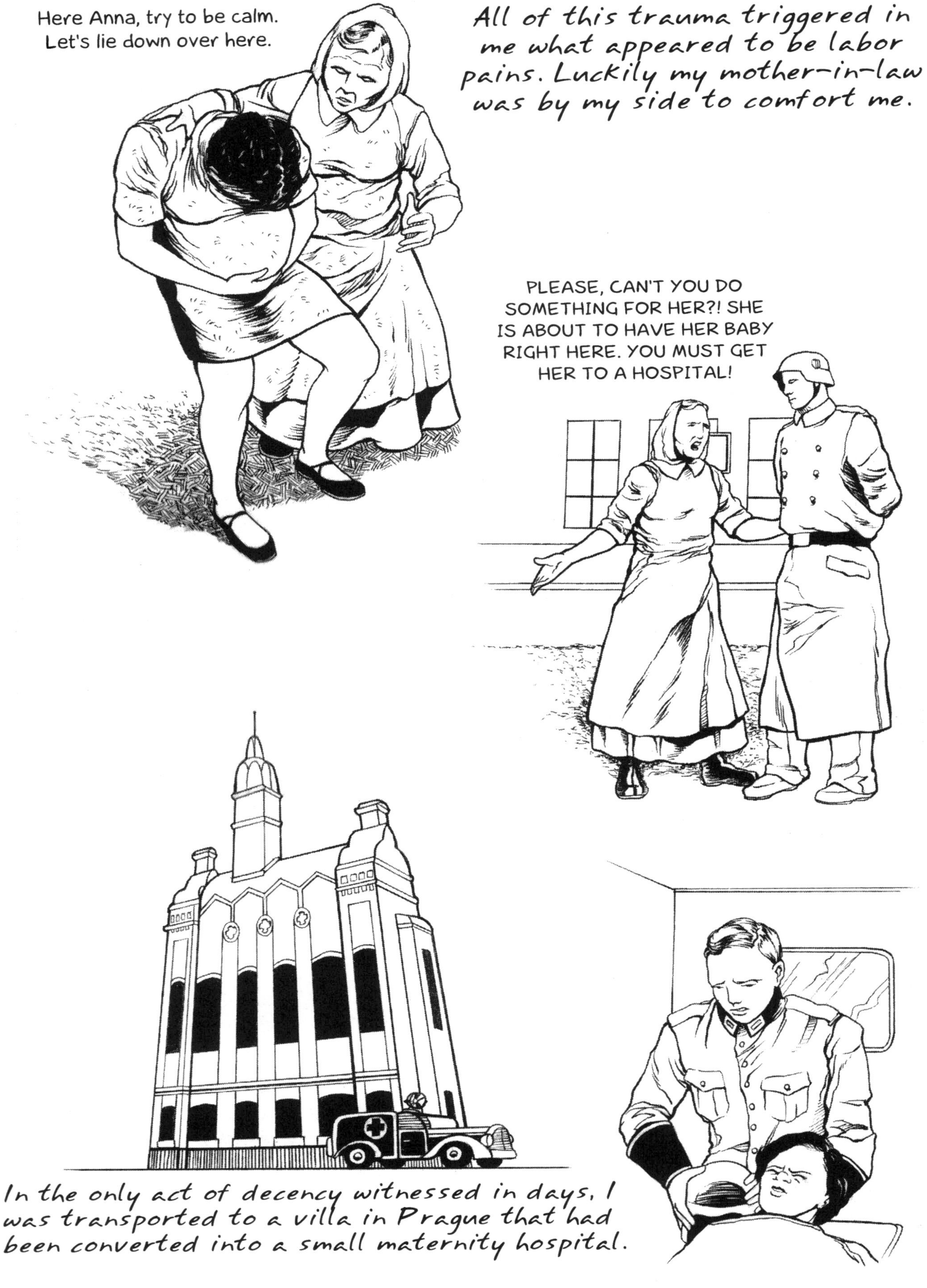
Here Anna, try to be calm. Let's lie down over here.
All of this trauma triggered in me what appeared to be labor pains. Luckily my mother-in-law was by my side to comfort me.
PLEASE, CAN'T YOU DO SOMETHING FOR HER?! SHE IS ABOUT TO HAVE HER BABY RIGHT HERE. YOU MUST GET HER TO A HOSPITAL!
In the only act of decency witnessed in days, I was transported to a villa in Prague that had been converted into a small maternity hospital.

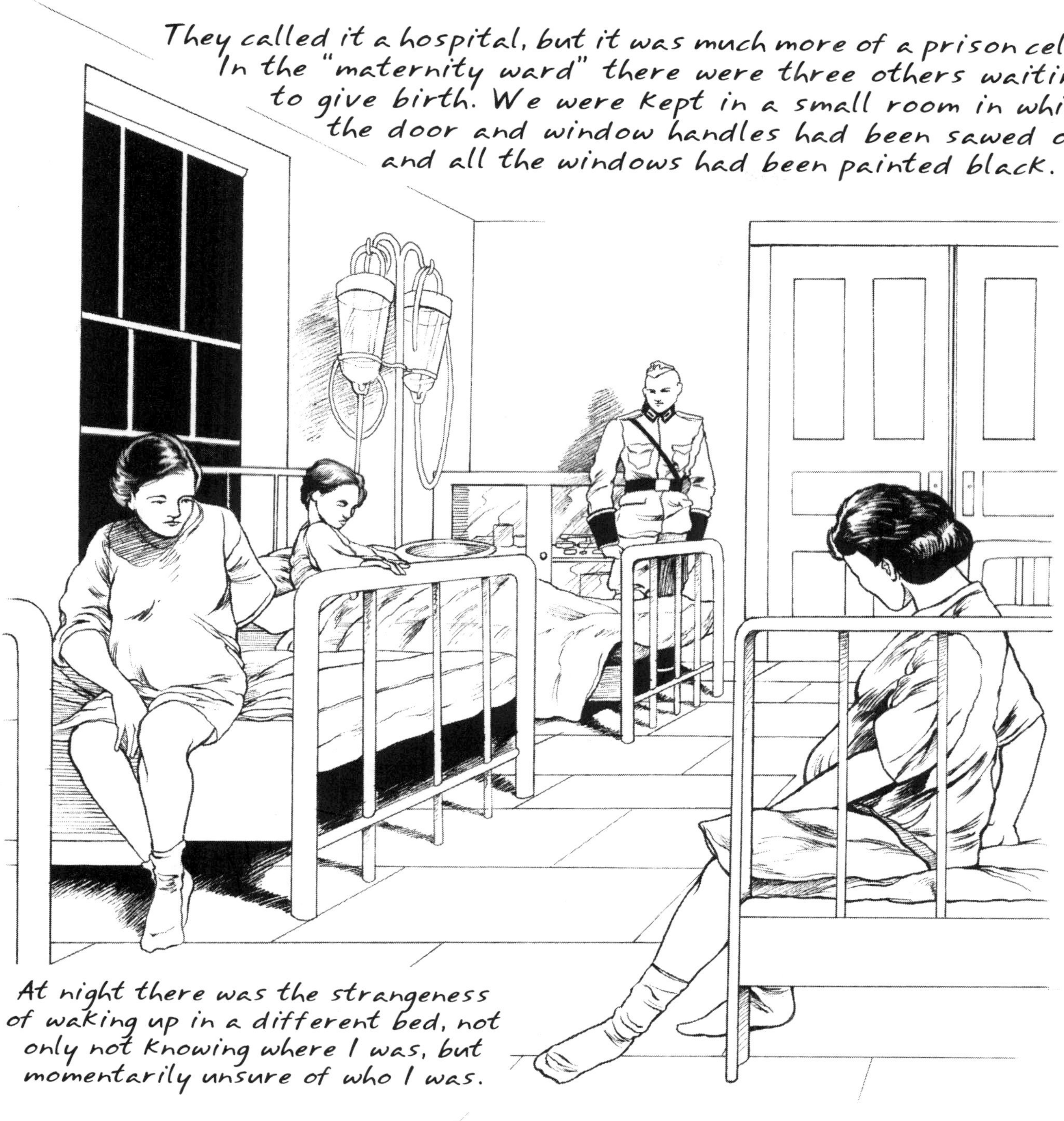
They called it a hospital, but it was much more of a prison cell. In the "maternity ward" there were three others waiting to give birth. We were kept in a small room in which the door and window handles had been sawed off and all the windows had been painted black.
At night there was the strangeness of waking up in a different bed, not only not knowing where I was, but momentarily unsure of who I was.

The air was stale and close as we waited for labor, unable to communicate for fear of being beaten by the guards who watched us at all times. Whenever the realization that I was being kept alive only to produce a healthy baby struck me, I quickly tried to push the thought from my mind.

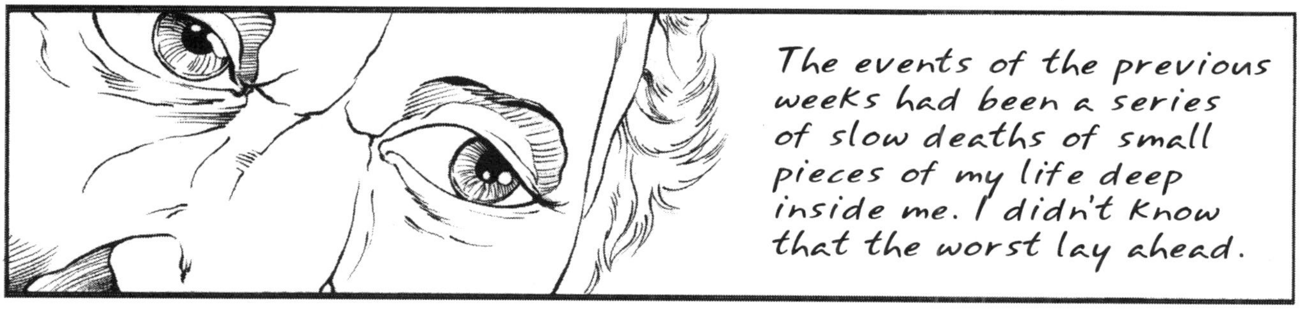
The events of the previous weeks had been a series of slow deaths of small pieces of my life deep inside me. I didn't know that the worst lay ahead.

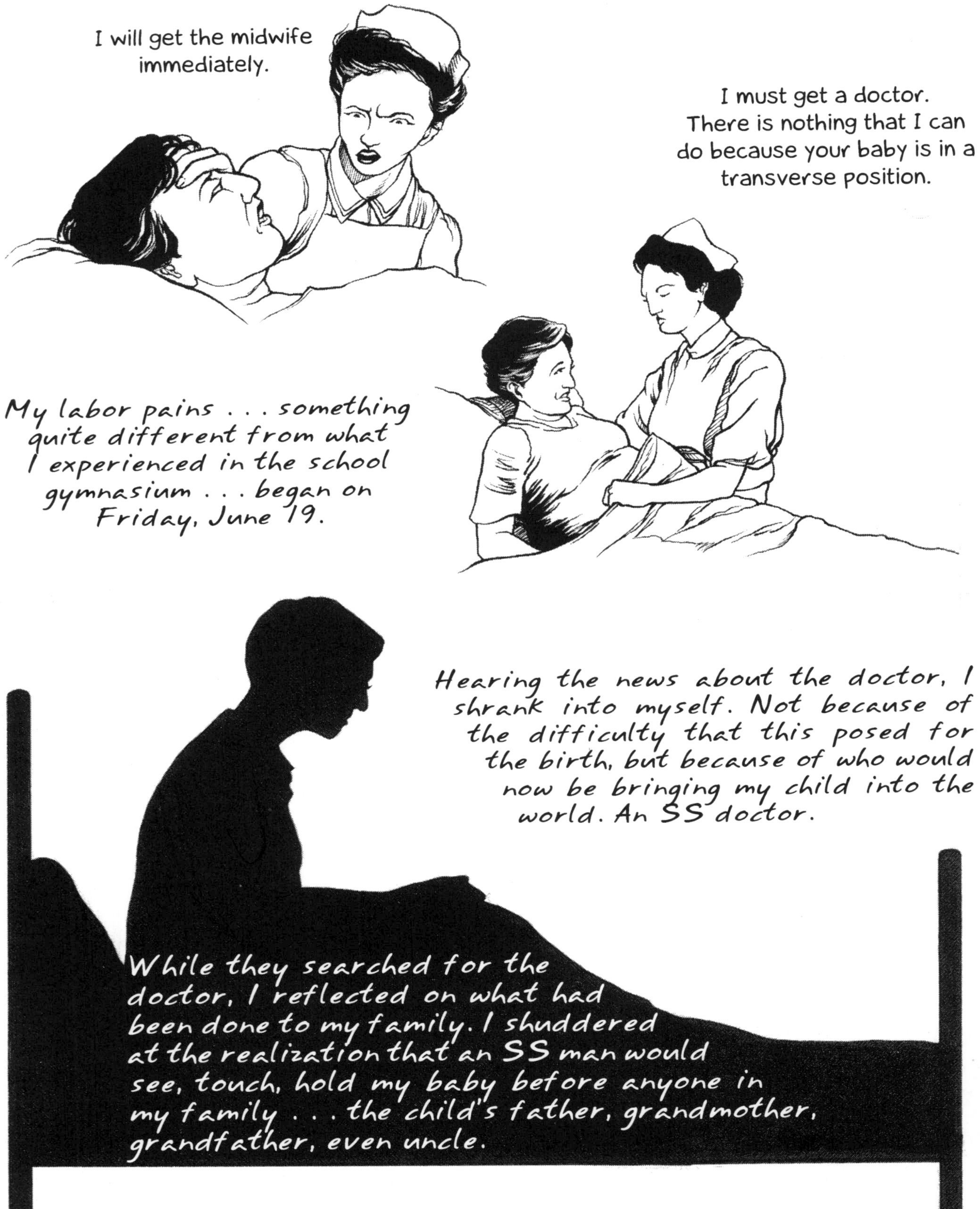

I will get the midwife immediately.

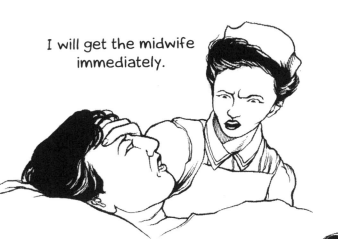

I must get a doctor. There is nothing that I can do because your baby is in a transverse position.

My labor pains . . . something quite different from what I experienced in the school gymnasium . . . began on Friday, June 19.

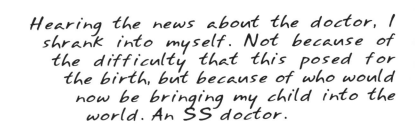

Hearing the news about the doctor, I shrank into myself. Not because of the difficulty that this posed for the birth, but because of who would now be bringing my child into the world. An SS doctor.

While they searched for the doctor, I reflected on what had been done to my family. I shuddered at the realization that an SS man would see, touch, hold my baby before anyone in my family . . . the child's father, grandmother, grandfather, even uncle.

All this raced through my head during my labor pains. Suddenly my path became clear. I would not let him touch my baby. I felt a surge of strength come from my decision . . . I would give birth alone. I could sense that my family were there with me, lending me courage. I grasped the cold metal bed rails and gave birth to my daughter.

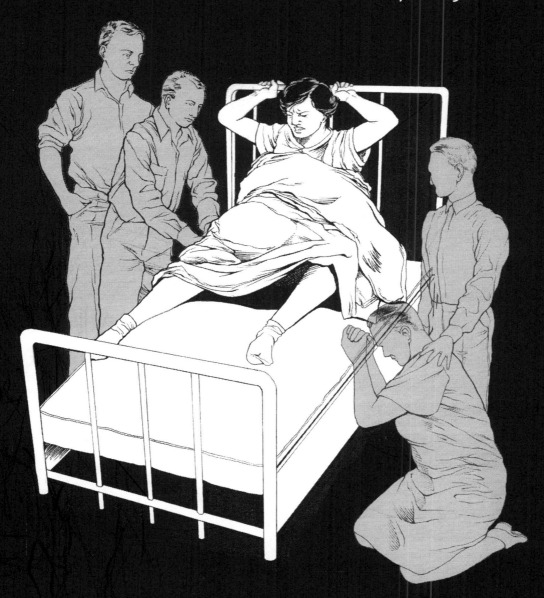

I don't remember crying or pain, only the rush of joy at holding this small being of innocence and beauty in an environment permeated with ugliness and hate. I was alive and so was she.

I named you Venceslava, after your father Vaclav. There was much of him in you. You were tall and thin like him. You had his soulful eyes. I still recall entire days spent during that brief period we had together simply gazing into your eyes as you looked around trying to comprehend the world you had joined.

For close to a month, our lives in the hospital were as normal as the times allowed...

...spending precious days with you while always fearful of the Germans who were watching us.

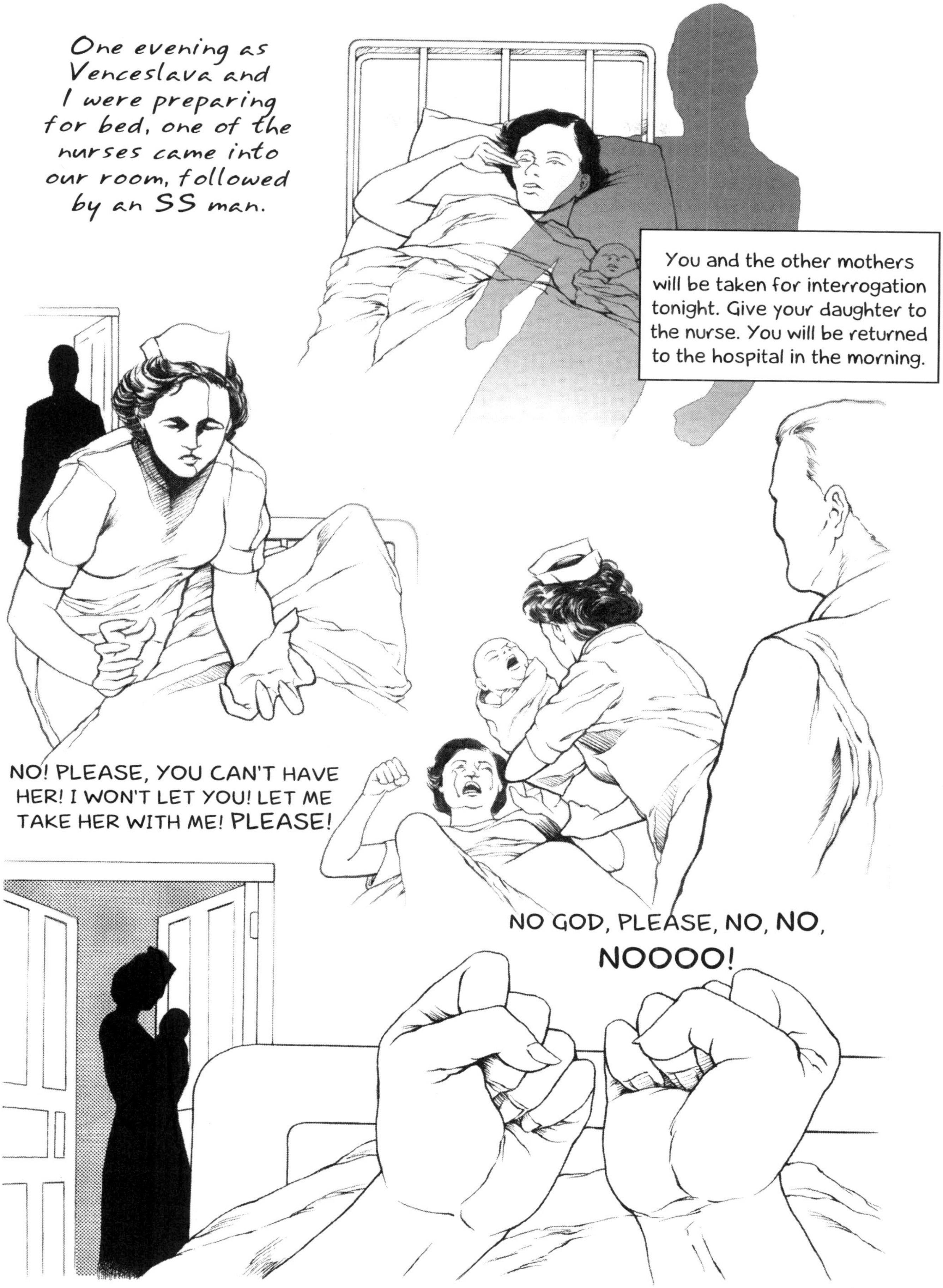
One evening as Venceslava and I were preparing for bed, one of the nurses came into our room, followed by an SS man.
You and the other mothers will be taken for interrogation tonight. Give your daughter to the nurse. You will be returned to the hospital in the morning.
NO! PLEASE, YOU CAN'T HAVE HER! I WON'T LET YOU! LET ME TAKE HER WITH ME! PLEASE!
NO GOD, PLEASE, NO, NO, NOOOO!

I'm sorry, could I take a moment. This is more difficult than I anticipated. It's been a long time since I've said these things out loud to anyone.

Please take as long as you need.

If all of this is too difficult for you, we can stop at any time.

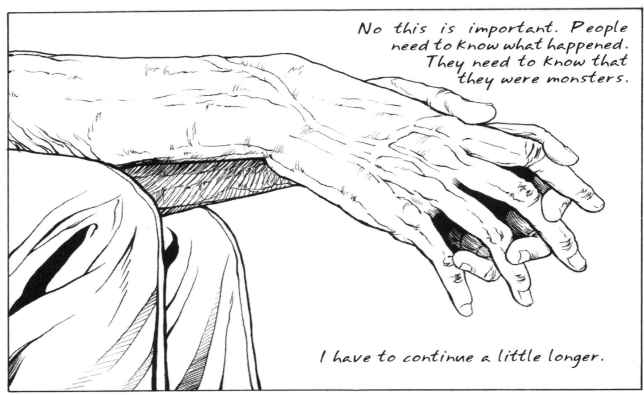

No this is important. People need to know what happened. They need to know that they were monsters.

I have to continue a little longer.

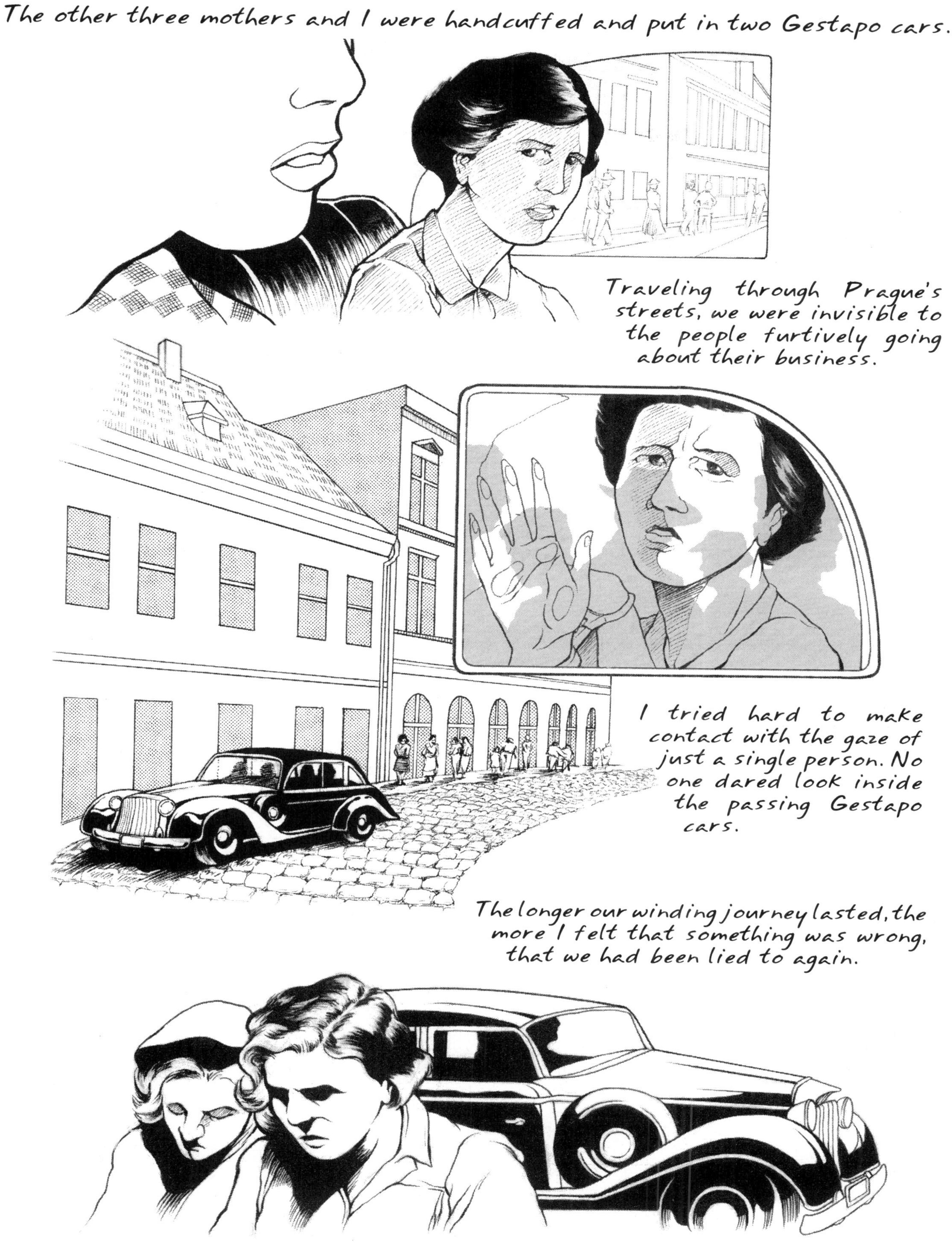
The other three mothers and I were handcuffed and put in two Gestapo cars.
Traveling through Prague's streets, we were invisible to the people furtively going about their business.
I tried hard to make contact with the gaze of just a single person. No one dared look inside the passing Gestapo cars.
The longer our winding journey lasted, the more I felt that something was wrong, that we had been lied to again.

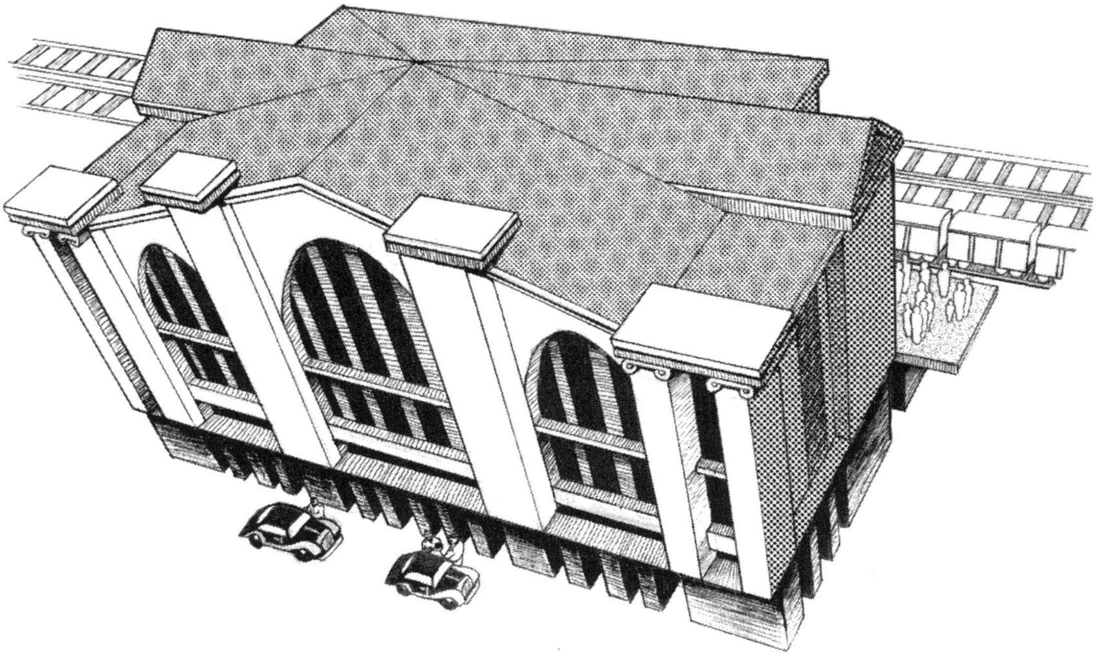

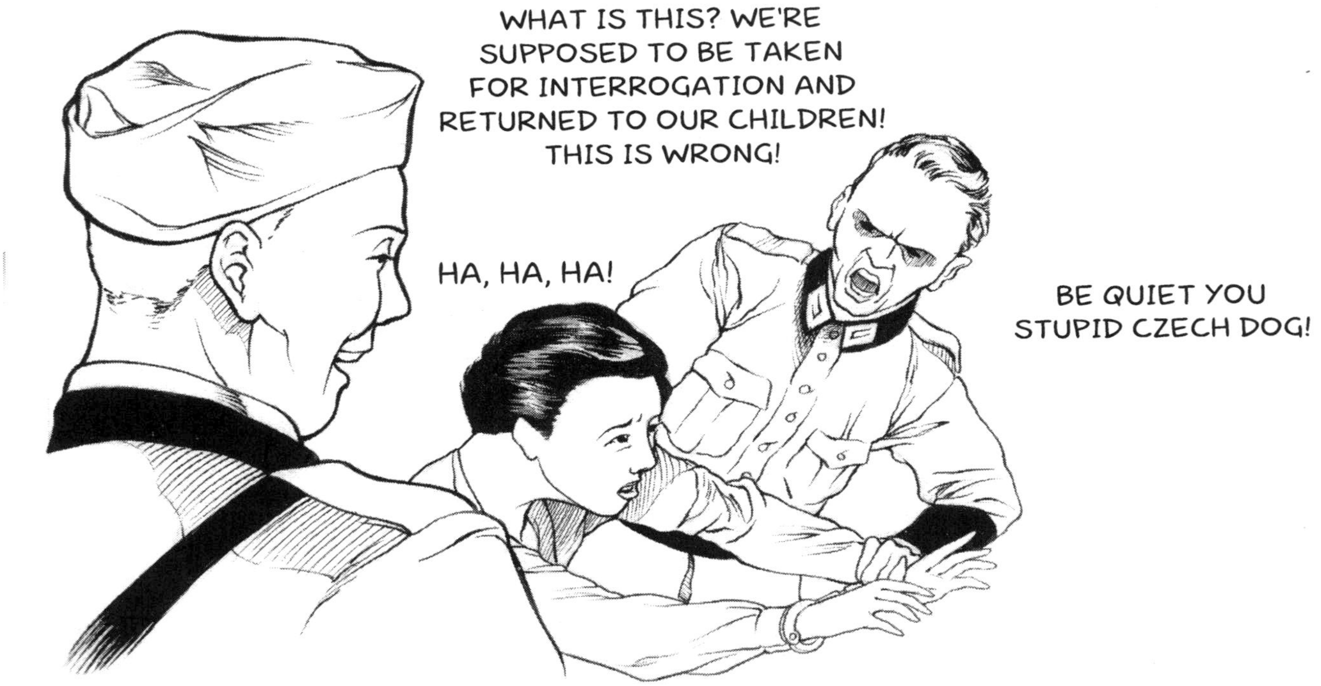
WHAT IS THIS? WE'RE SUPPOSED TO BE TAKEN FOR INTERROGATION AND RETURNED TO OUR CHILDREN! THIS IS WRONG!
HA, HA, HA!
BE QUIET YOU STUPID CZECH DOG!

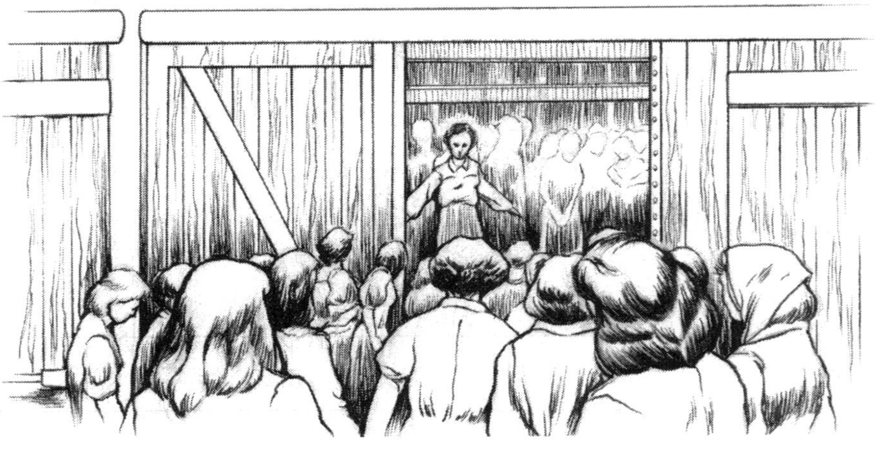

I'm sorry . . . I should probably stop now after all.

I thought that I could do this, but it is becoming more difficult than I expected.

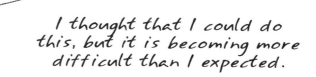

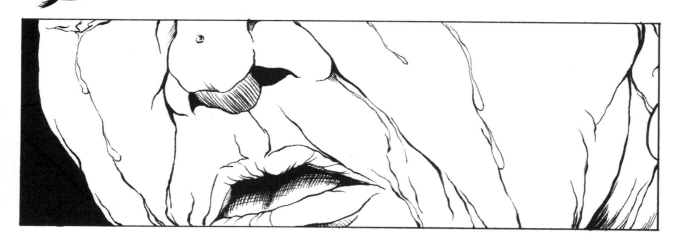

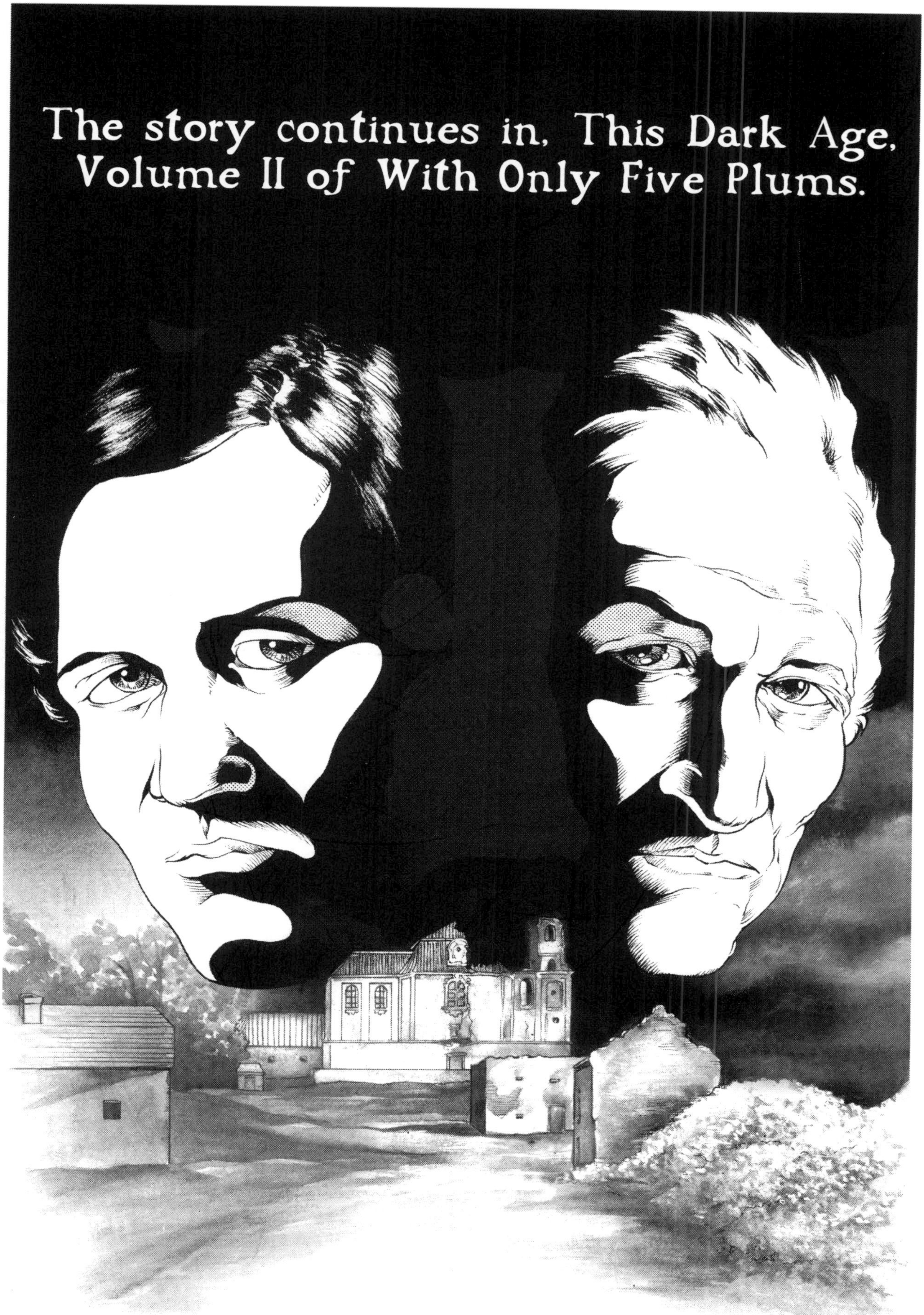
The story continues in, This Dark Age,
Volume II of With Only Five Plums.

JONATHON'S SKETCHBOOK

OLD AND YOUNG ANNA

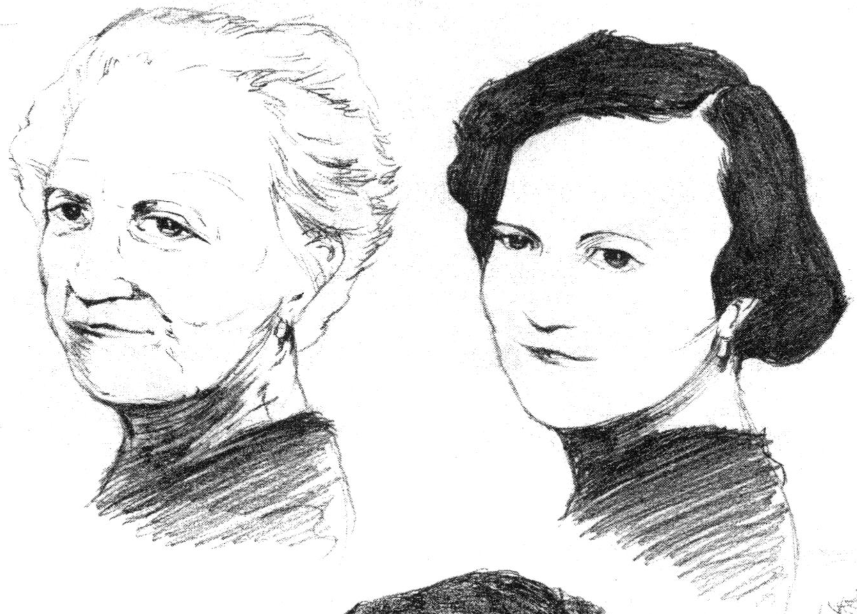

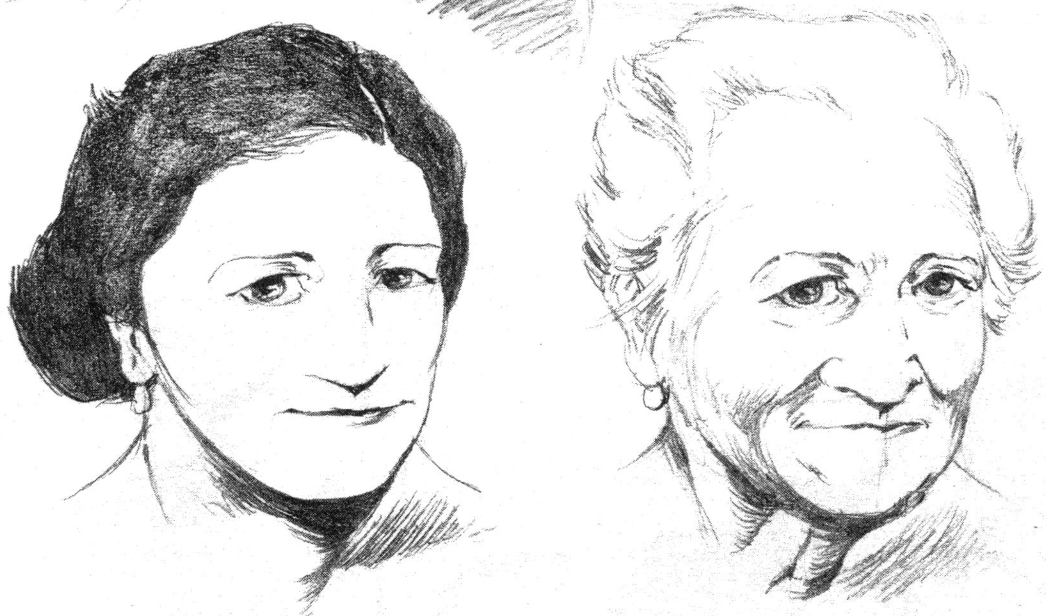

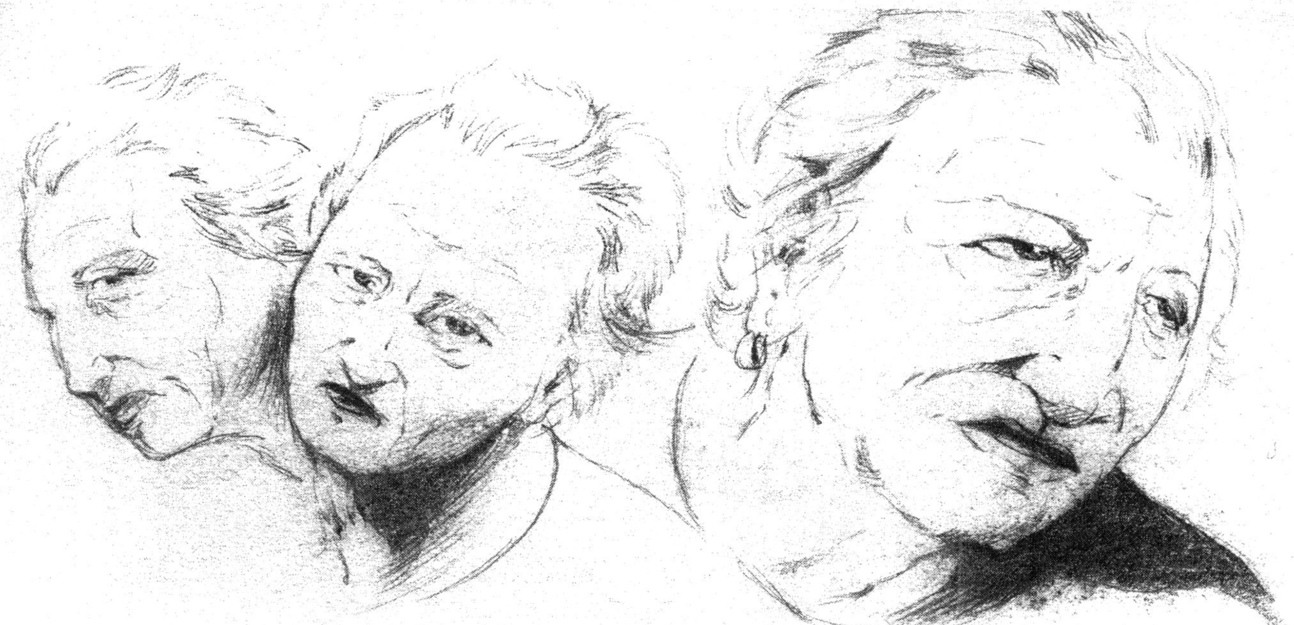

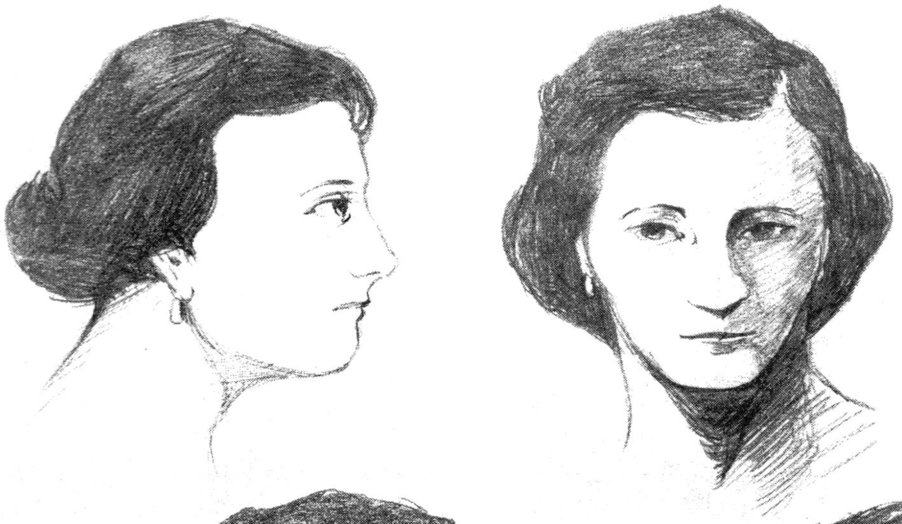

ANNA

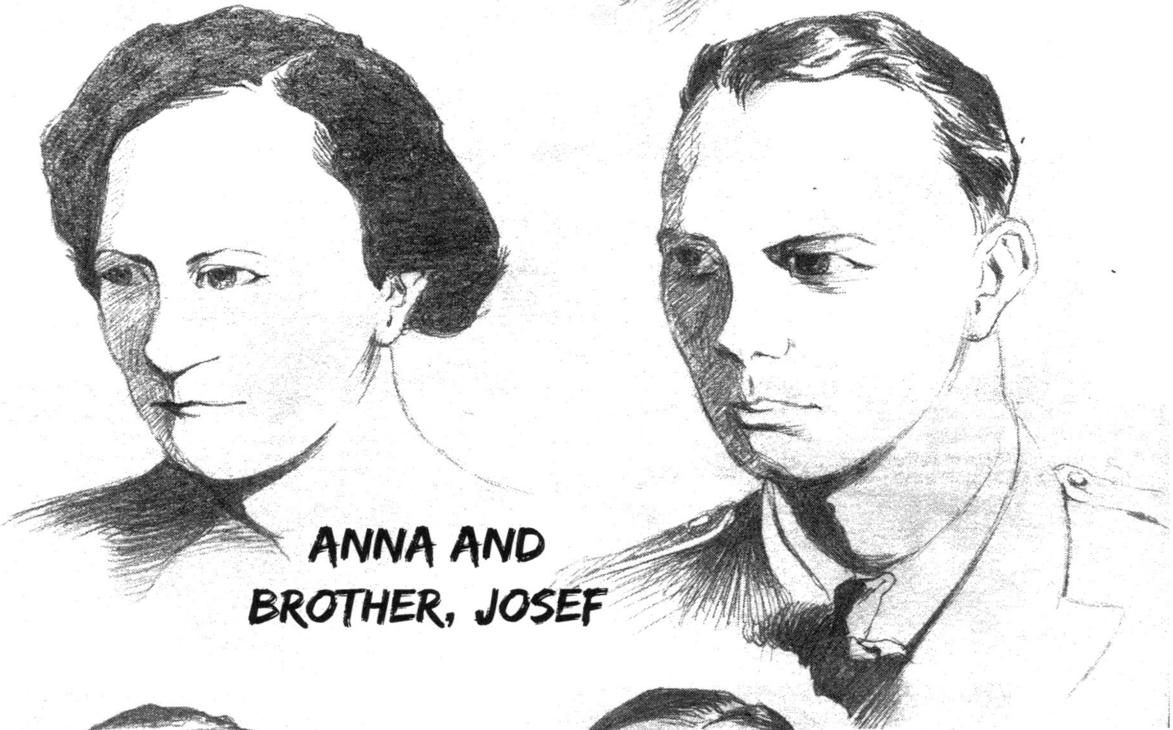

ANNA AND BROTHER, JOSEF

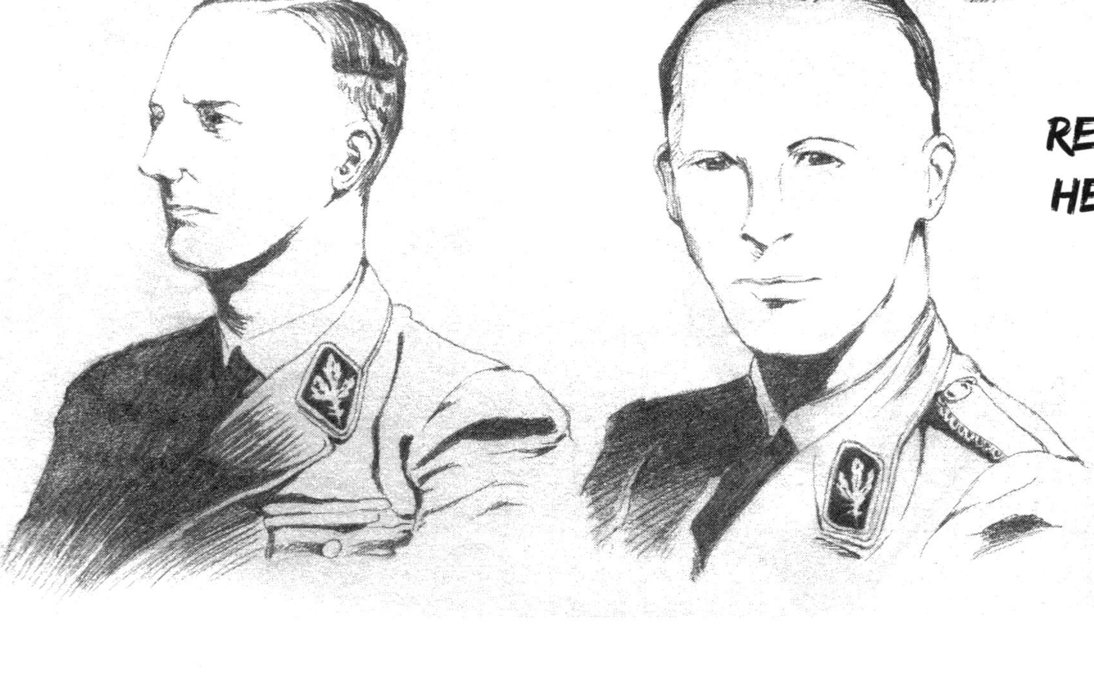

REINHARD HEYDRICH

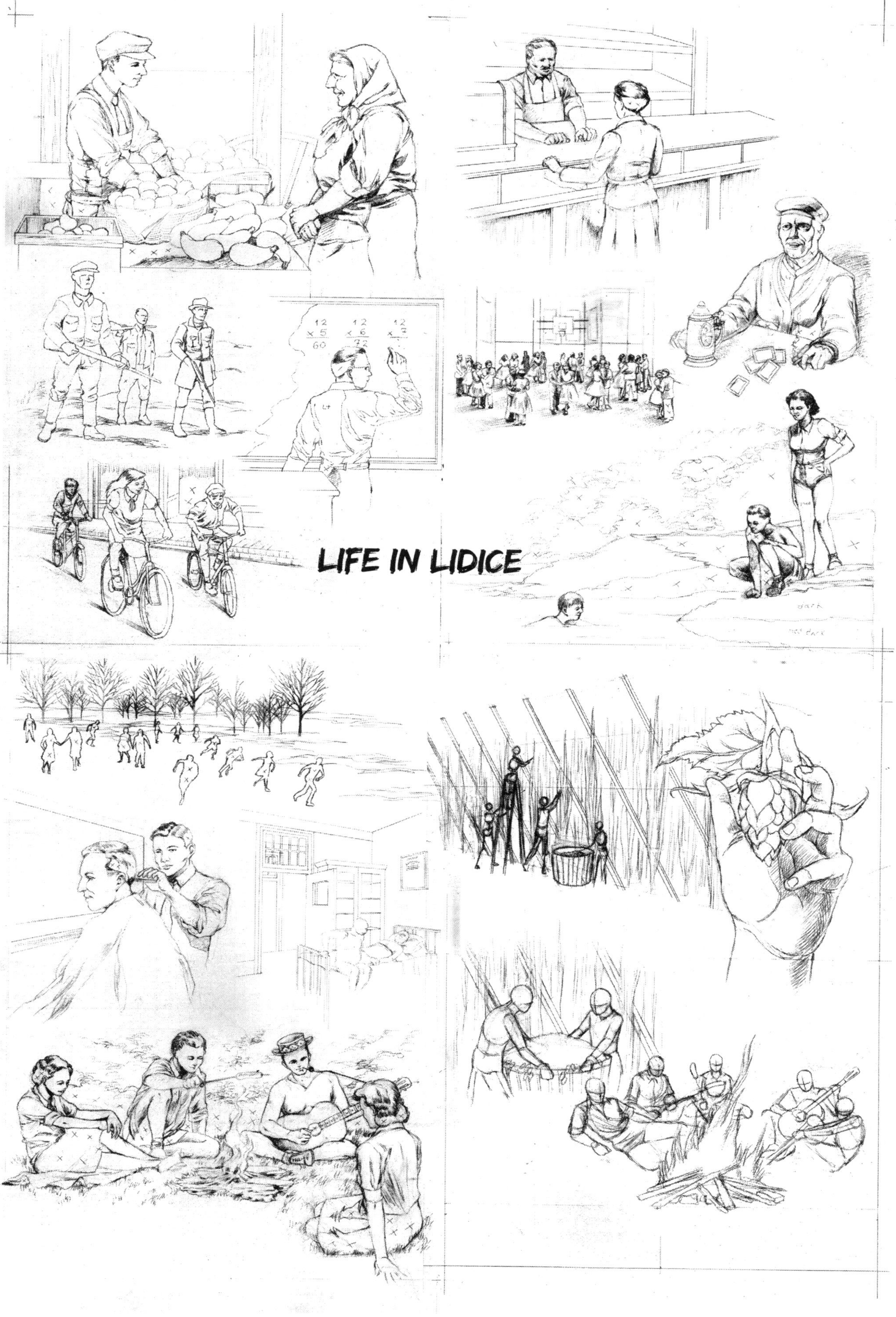
LIFE IN LIDICE

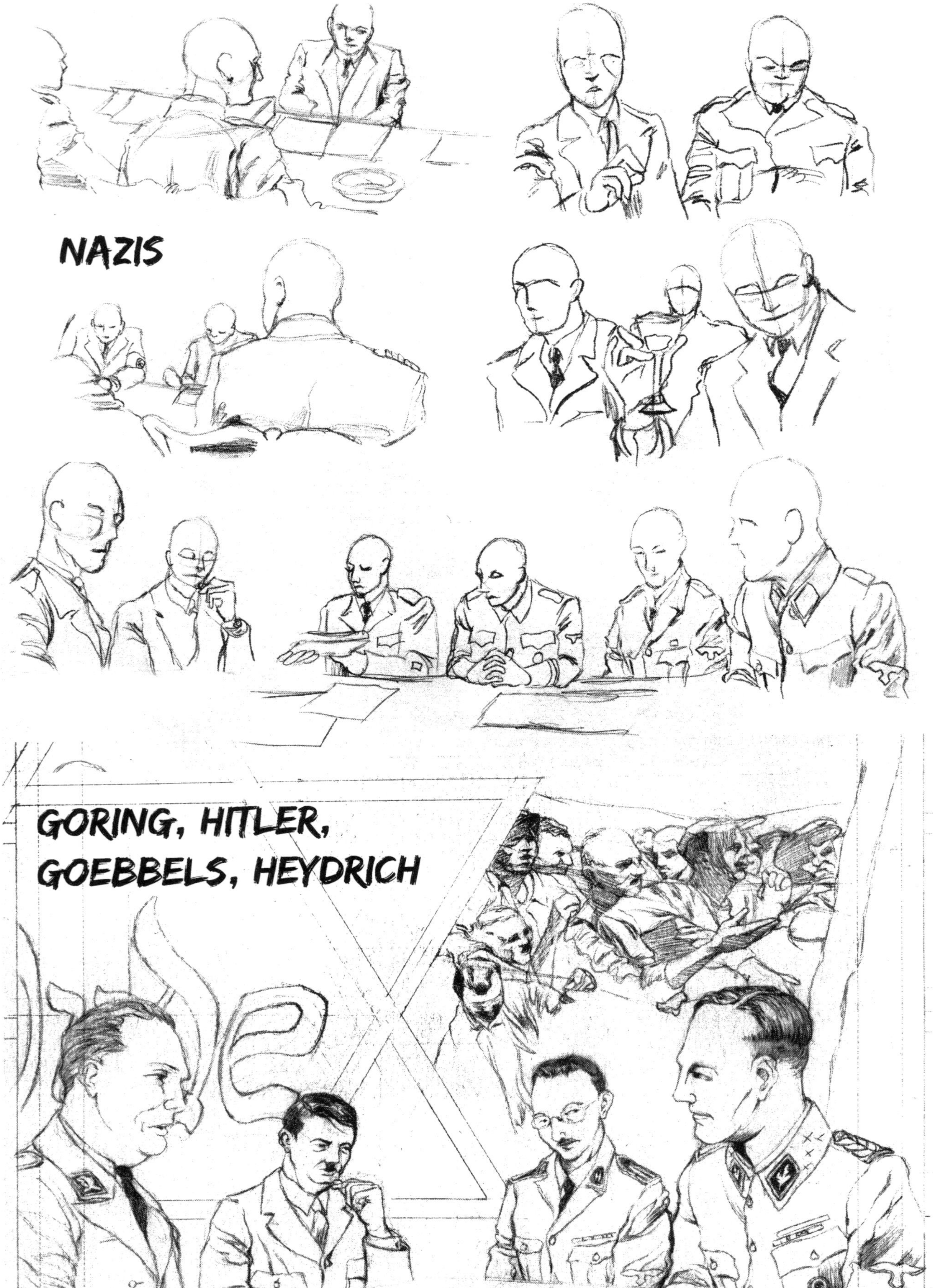
NAZIS
GORING, HITLER,
GOEBBELS, HEYDRICH

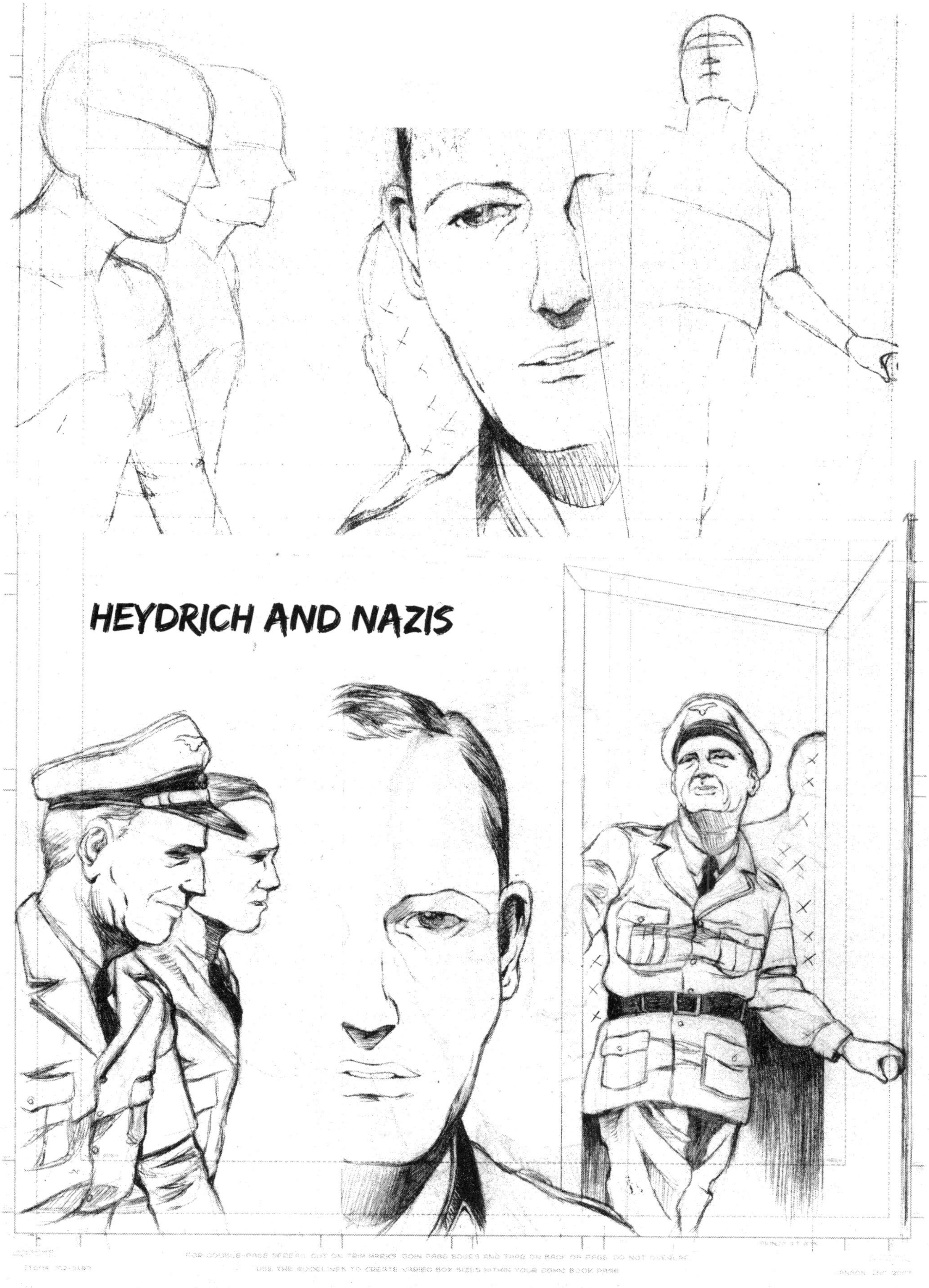
HEYDRICH AND NAZIS

ORIGINAL COVER

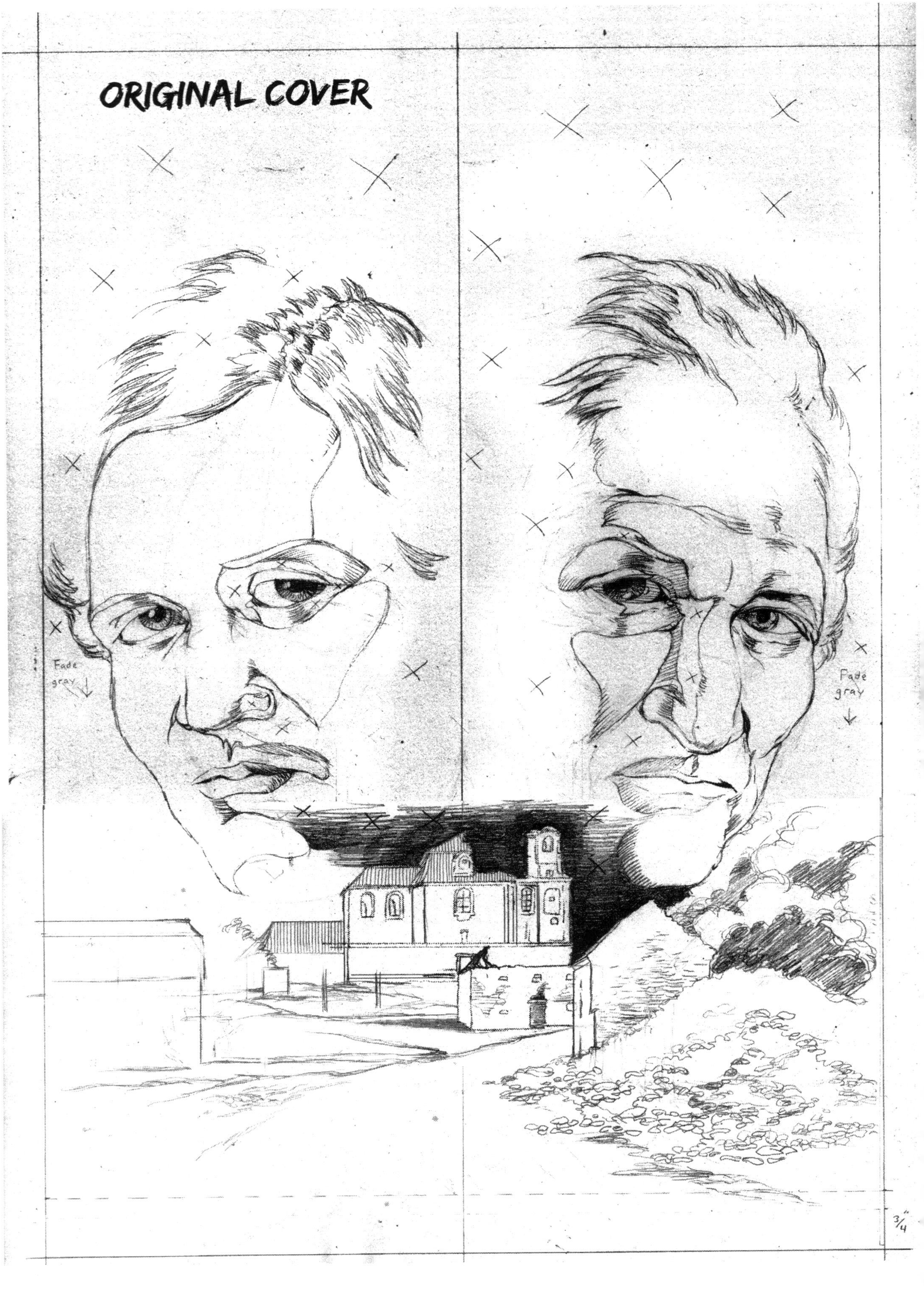
Fade gray
Fade gray
3/4"

Acknowledgments—T.E.

There are a number of people without whom this project would not have been possible.

Pavel Minarik was instrumental in helping me find and interview Anna Nesporova.

Translation of the original interview tapes was done by Magda Pintarova.

Thanks to Jonathon for his beautiful art and his patience in dealing with my sometimes less than clear vision of the images on the page.

John Petro and Susan S.R. Petro provided invaluable legal advice.

Thanks are due to Tim Jacoby for his early assistance with Adobe InDesign and to John Novak and Liz Neal for creating my website.

I am grateful for my parents' love and encouragement.

Finally, I would not have even started this book without the gentle prodding nor finished it without the constant support of my wife, Michelle.

Acknowledgments—J.R.

Thanks are due to the many artistic influences that helped shape this book, among them: illustrators Victor Ambrus, Will Eisner, and George Perez, as well as film directors Paul Wegener, Frank Pierson, John Carpenter, Adam Bernstein, Jonathan Demme, and Walter Hill. Special thanks are due to comics legend Joe Kubert, whose book Yossel served as the template for much of this work.

Thanks to Terry, for taking a chance on this untested sales clerk from his local art supply store. I wouldn't be the artist I am today without his patience and challenging spirit.

Thanks to the men and women of the Sunday Comix Group, who provided endless support and insightful critiques during the completion of this book. They have been with me since the beginning and are with me still .

Most of all, thanks to Martha Parsons Seiter, my grandmother, without whose love and support this project would have never happened as it did. To her I dedicate this work.

Sources

Lidice. Rostislav Kocourek. Orbis, 1972

Lidice. Eleanor Wheeler. Orbis, 1962

Lidice: A Tribute by Members of the International P.E.N. G. Allen & Unwin, 1944

Lidice: Sacrificial Village. John Bradley. Ballantine Books, 1972

Lidice: The Story of a Czech Village. Eduard Stehlik. Lidice Memorial, 2004

Memories of Lidice. Eduard Stehlik. Lidice Memorial, 2007

The Road to Hell: Recollections of the Nazi Death March. Joseph Freeman. Paragon House, 1998

Ravensbruck: Everyday Life in a Women's Concentration Camp 1939-45. Markus Wiener Publishers, 2000

The Lidice Memorial. http://www.lidice_memorial.cz/default_en.aspx